1

The
Quilters'
Cookbook

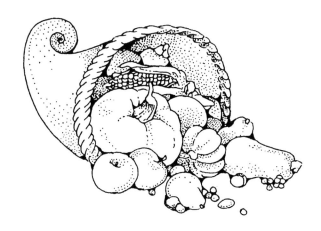

© Barbara Soden 2009

Any recipe in this book that involves canning should not be considered to be complete. The user of this book should consult other resources to learn the techniques and dangers involved in home canning.

I am dedicating this book to my late mother Dorothy Louise Hanselman (1912-2007), who always supported my endeavors. I miss you Mom!!

And to my two nieces, Amy Borley and Karen Hanselman, who have always been a bright spot in my life.

Cherry Crisp - Delicious - Pg. 166

While doing research for this book, I found that quilting was a lot more complicated then I envisioned. I had no idea of what went into making one so a friend and neighbor, Betty Treasure, was kind enough to show me some of the quilts she has made over the years, and give me a short course in quilting.

One of Betty's quilts was a southwest story quilt. It was made with scraps from her children's outgrown clothes so that had an even more special meaning. The rich colors and textures gave it a vibrant look and upon a closer look I could see the delicate stitches, done by hand, tracing patterns on the quilt.

I have since spoken to many other quilters and got much more insight into the quilting process plus some of their favorite recipes. I hope you enjoy this novices' first voyage into the world of quilting. I've enjoyed it very much and have learned a lot from all the kind people who took the time to talk with me.

A WORLD OF QUILTS

CIVIL WAR AND ABOLITION QUILTS

The Civil War started in 1861 and promised to be of short duration. Both sides felt they could clean up the other and come back home in a jiffy. However, it was not meant to be, and it lasted four long years.

The women in their fervor to be patriotic sewed clothes, knitted scarves and made many things to keep the soldiers happy. They held fairs and bazaars and quilts were a favorite item to raise funds for the cause. It was frowned upon then for women to be involved in any commercial enterprise but they wanted to be part of the war effort so they continued to raise money.

Women created beautiful, colorful quilts with Log Cabin patterns, Flags quilts were also popular. There were Album and Gunboat quilts often made from silk scraps.

Northern women were used to meeting together and quilting and sewing for the church and abolitionist groups so making quilts were fairly easy for them. Southern women were not accustomed to sewing as the wealthier women had slaves to do their sewing for them. However, they soon learned and made quilts and blankets until their fabrics became scarce. Southern communities competed to see who could raise the most money for supplies and ships.

The south was blockaded so ships could not get in to deliver goods. Eventually textiles became so expensive that women had to make do with materials that they spun themselves.

In late 1862 they stopped making clothes and quilts and they felt the funds collected should go for medical supplies. And instead of auctioning off the quilts, they were made and sent to the soldiers and were made from any available fabrics.

In 1865 the war was coming to a close and the anti-slavery movement was taking shape. Quilts were said to be used to help the slaves escape along the Underground Railroad. A particular quilt hanging in a window indicated a safe house. This is not proven to be true and could possibly be a bit of folklore, but it does add some interest to the history of quilts.

AUTOGRAPH QUILTS

There are two distinctive types of autograph quilts. The simpler, single pattern quilts are known as Friendship Quilts. They usually consist of a simple block pattern and are often made from scraps.

The Sampler Album Quilts and more formal and made up of unique, complicated blocks often appliquéd or pieced. Both have the same tradition of signed remembrances.

Signatures were written with indelible ink or embroidered. If a person in the quilting group had a particularly beautiful handwriting they would do all the signatures.

These blocks were often made by a single woman using scraps from her friends who would sign their names on each block. Another way of doing an autograph quilt was to have each woman make a block then the whole group would get together and put them together and then quilt. Either way they were lovely blankets and treasured among families.

These quilts were used to record memories of dear friends and family. They were made to give to a friend who was going to leave the community and move to faraway places as a remembrance of their former home. These were quilts that the owners cherished and often it was the only family contact they had. When a dear one passed away the name on the quilt became more precious than ever.

CRAZY QUILTS

"Crazies" was what the Victorian era magazines called these quilts. In the late 1800's the Japanese created clever ceramics with asymmetrical shapes. They were shown at the Philadelphia Centennial Exposition and the quitters found this fascinating and incorporated this look into their quilts.

The quilts were usually small, unquilted lap robes. They were more for decoration than function. The wealthier women of the times were able to afford the rich silks and velvets as they had the time and money to spend. As time went on, the fabrics used became more traditional - denim, flannel, and cotton.

These quilts were carefully planned and the pieces were triangles and other odd shapes. Many hours were spent arranging and rearranging the pieces to get the most interesting look. They were delicately stitched in decorative stitches with names like herringbone, chain, feather and others. There were often pictures painted on the quilt and then embroidered. They are also used to record favorite family events.

These quilts were popular until the early 1900's then the enthusiasm died down. The earlier quilts made with silks and brocades are deteriorating now as the fabric used contained metals to give them weight. Preservationists are trying to save the old quilts but are fighting a losing battle. In the future they will only be seen in photographs.

AFRICAN AMERICAN QUILTS

Most of the textiles originally used in Africa, were made by the men. It was important to recognize tribes and hunting parties. They wanted to be seen from afar and used large shapes and bright colors. When slaves were brought to the United States women took over the tradition.

After the Civil War many African American women worked in homes as domestics. It was a hard life and there was little time for entertainment such as quilting. Quilts were made out of necessity and any scraps or old clothing were used to make them. Many quilts were made with strips of fabric and called "string" quilts. This was a quick way of making a quilt and very efficient.

Story quilts told of ancestors and life in the roots of African settlers. These techniques have been handed down through generations and were sometimes called folk quilts. They told a story with appliqué and embroidery and are still made today.

Before textiles were available through merchants, the African American slave women would spin, sew and quilt, often weaving their own fabric. Their masters' families used the quilts they made and they had little time for doing any sewing for their own families.

After the 1920's patterns were available through magazines and newspapers and fabric was easy to get and relatively inexpensive.

They used large patterns with strong, bold colors representative of their African roots. Few of these quilts can be found today.

As industrialization came into being it gave new opportunities for employment. Women found that they had little time to quilt after working their day jobs. When they retired they found quilting anew and by that time magazine patterns were very popular so their quilting became more of the mainstream and less of their heritage.

CHINTZ APPLIQUÉ

Chintz Appliqué is also known as broderie perse which in French means Persian embroidery. This was a popular technique done mainly by affluent women in England. The first chintz fabrics were imported to England from India about 1600. Many consumers didn't find them appealing so the Indian textile producers designed prints with floral themes from English artwork. Oriental motifs were also popular. It was quite a mix of east and west.

England feared that their silk and wool trades would be hurt by the import of the fabrics so the put a ban on the import of printed cottons. The cost became prohibitive and women had to find new ways of getting and using the treasured fabrics. They found that cutting out the patterns from these prints and then appliquéing them to a less expensive fabric would prolong the usage. This is where technique of broderie perse came into favor.

When people came to this country they carried on the tradition and were eager to use these prints but fabric was scarce. The husbands would pick up a yard or two of this cloth when they were in New York or one of the other big cities. They were then appliquéd on homespun fabrics.

These "quilts" were more for show than use. Some were used unlined as summer spreads and others were layered and quilted. They were well kept and preserved and many wonderful examples remain today in museums and private collections.

DEPRESSION ERA QUILTS

During the Depression, magazines used quilting patterns as a way to sell magazines. Hard times didn't sell magazines and this gave hope that life will go on.

This was a practical activity women could do to satisfy her creativity and also keep her family warm. The patterns and colors added beauty and color to an often drab existence. Little expense was involved as scraps were used from outgrown clothing and linens.

Selling quilts were often a way to help a family get by. Many women did piecework for pay. Many times it was the work of several women – one would sew the blocks together, another quilted it and still another would sew on the binding. These were often done by hand which made them even more valuable.

The Depression was a time to go back to the basics so quilting was a way of reviving the past, safer times.

1920's REVIVAL QUILTS

The 20's were boom years and the American public became fascinated with Colonial antiques and quilts. Magazines published patterns from the era and women were eager to make quilts reminiscent of the times. It was a romanticized vision of the past but colonial furniture and quilts were very popular.

The quilters, new and old, wanted pastel and light colored fabrics that were new at that time. They wanted a remembrance of their heritage but also the new up-to-date fabrics. With the softer colors and embroidery stitches, it became an art form.

The revival of quilting sparked interest in city women as a new craft to challenge them. Rural women had always made quilts and sewed but now we're finding new creative ways to quilt. All were delighted with the new fabrics and what they could do with them. The colors were dreamy and romantic and offered a more diversified selection of fabrics. It was a whole new era.

NATIVE AMERICAN QUILTS

Native Americans have very diverse cultures. Each tribe has a certain area where they live and have their individual symbolism representative of each group. The artwork is evident in leather gods, rugs and intricate beadwork.

When the settlers and missionaries came to live among the Indians they brought their quilts and the Native Americans found them fascinating and soon found ways to incorporate their own designs into their own quilts.

The patchwork was also used in other ways. The traditional dress for ceremonies was woven into cloth to make blouses and skirts for the Seminoles. The southwest Native Americans used the designs in their blankets and baskets for the quilt patterns.

These quilts were an important of their lives. They were given for gifts, ceremonies, funerals and any other occasion. It was treasured and considered the perfect gift.

TABLE OF CONTENTS

BREAD AND MUFFIN RECIPES

WREN HOUSE

TABLE OF CONTENTS

BEDE'S CAST IRON CORNBREAD

4 c. cornmeal
2 tsp. baking soda
2 tsp. salt
4 eggs, beaten
4 c. milk (buttermilk can be substituted)
¼ c. sugar
½ c. butter or margarine, melted

Heat cast iron pan until very hot. In the meantime, combine dry ingredients and make a well in the center. Combine liquid ingredients and pour into well. Blend until mixed well.

Pour batter into heated pan and bake at 425 degrees for 35-45 minutes until knife inserted in center comes out clean. Top should be golden brown.

NOTE: Bacon drippings can be used in place of the butter or margarine for an entirely different flavor.

Corn kernels and/or chopped green chiles can be added also.

CRACKLIN' CORNBREAD

2 c. cornmeal
½ tsp. baking powder
1 tsp. salt
2 c. buttermilk
1 egg, beaten
2 c. cracklins
½ c. flour
2 T. sugar
1 tsp. baking soda

Combine cornmeal, flour, baking powder, salt and baking soda. Add buttermilk and egg, mix well. Add cracklins and pour mixture into a greased cast iron skillet and bake at 400° for 30 minutes or until brown.

Cracklins are fried pork rinds and are highly treasured in the south.

LEMON BASIL MUFFINS

1 c. flour
1 c. whole wheat flour
2 tsps. baking powder
2 T. plum jam
1 c. milk
1 egg
1 T. vegetable oil
2 T. dried basil
1 T. lemon juice

Combine flours, baking powder and sugar. Combine other ingredients in a separate bowl. Mix ingredients together and stir only until dry ingredients are moistened.

Bake at 400° for 20 minutes or until a toothpick inserted comes out clean. Makes 12 muffins.

BLUE BIRD

GREEN CHILE ONION BREAD

6 6oz. frozen demi loaf
bread (rise and bake)

2 sm. sweet onions
1-1/2 c. jalapeños, seeded
and diced

Remove loaves from freezer, spray lightly with oil and cover with plastic wrap. Thaw overnight in the refrigerator. Julienne the onions and sauté in butter over low heat until caramelized. Remove from heat and let cool.

Wearing gloves, dice chiles and add to the onion mixture, mix well. Divide mixture into 6 parts and cut into bread dough to incorporate. Reshape dough into loaves. Rise and bake for 30 minutes at the temperature listed on the dough.

PECAN AND RED ONION BREAD
For Bread Maker

1 pkg. yeast
2 c. bread flour
1-1/2 tsp. sugar
1-1/2 tsp. salt
3/4 c. pecans, chopped

1 c. + 1 T. warm milk
1/4 c. butter or margarine,
  melted
1/2 c. red onion, chopped

All ingredients should be at room temperature. Combine in bread maker in given order. Select white bread on bread maker and start.

SHOO FLY

BLUEBERRY NUT BREAD

1 pt. blueberries, rinsed but not dried
3 c. plus 3 T. whole wheat flour, divided
2 c. sugar
½ c. vegetable oil
1 tsp. baking soda
1 tsp. salt
1 c. pecans, chopped
4 eggs
1 tsp. cinnamon

In a medium bowl, combine the blueberries and 3 T. flour..
Toss to coat. In a large bowl, combine the remaining
ingredients and mix well. Carefully fold in blueberries.

Spoon batter into greased and floured 9 x 5" loaf pans.
Bake for 55 minutes to 1 hour or until a toothpick inserted
into the center comes out clean. Allow to cool slightly then
remove to a wire rack to cool completely.

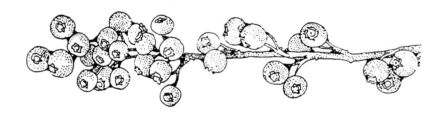

ONION ROLLS

2 T. olive oil
3 slices bacon, chopped
5 c. onions, sliced
½ c. black olives, chopped
12 brown and serve dinner rolls, or other rolls of your choice
1 c. Swiss cheese or smoked Gouda, grated

Cook bacon and onions for about 120 minutes until tender. Drain off fat. Slice rolls, keeping them connected and open out on a baking sheet.

Top with onion mixture and olives and sprinkle with cheese. Bake for 20 minutes at 400°. While still hot, fold rolls together.

CORN MUFFIN ONION BREAD

½ c. onions, chopped
2 T. butter or margarine
1 14 oz. pkg. corn muffin mix
½ c. sour cream
½ c. cheddar cheese, shredded

Sauté onions in butter until tender. Prepare corn muffin mix according to package directions. Pour into a greased 8 x 8 inch pan and top with onions. Mix sour cream and cheese together and spoon over top. Bake at 400° for 25 minutes.

SOUPS AND GUMBOS

LONE STAR

SAWTOOTH

34

TABLE OF CONTENTS

CHICKEN NOODLE SOUP

1 good-sized chicken
2 onions, diced
3 celery stalks, diced
3 carrots, sliced
4 qts. water
salt and pepper to taste

Clean and cut up chicken into bite sized pieces. Combine all ingredients in a large pot and bring to a boil. Reduce heat and simmer 2 to 2-1/2 hours. Add noodles and cook 15 minutes longer.

NOODLES:

2 eggs, beaten
1 c. flour
½ tsp. Salt

Combine all ingredients. Roll out or pat very thin. Let dry. Cut into thin strips and cook 15 minutes in chicken soup.

Noodles can be served alone. Just cook in boiling water for 15 minutes.

Ham and Okra Gumbo

2 T. butter or margarine
2 c. ham, chopped
1 onion, chopped
3 tomatoes, chopped
3 c. okra, sliced
3 potatoes, peeled and diced
2 stalks celery, diced
1 c. fresh corn, scraped from cob (or frozen)
salt and pepper to taste
water

Brown onion in butter or margarine until golden. Add other ingredients and cover with water and bring to a boil. Reduce heat and simmer, covered, about 45 minutes. *DO NOT OVERCOOK!*

TULIP

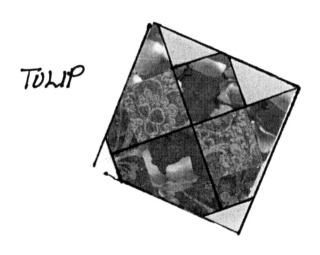

PEANUT (GOOBER) SOUP

1 c. peanuts
1 small onion, chopped
1 T. butter or margarine
3 c. water
salt and pepper to taste

Chop peanuts finely. In a pot, sauté onions in butter or margarine until golden brown. Stir peanuts into butter or margarine and add remaining ingredients. Bring to a boil, then reduce heat and simmer over low heat for ½ hour.

Goobers were common during the Civil War and they grew very well in the South because of the heat.

CREAMY PECAN SOUP

1-1/2 T. butter or margarine
3-1/2 c. onion, minced
6 T. tomato sauce
¾ c. pecans, ground to a paste
3 c. chicken broth
salt to taste
1/3 c. heavy cream
1 tsp. nutmeg
1 c. red wine or water

Melt butter or margarine over medium heat and add the onion. Cook until soft, stirring often. Add tomato sauce and continue cooking for about 2 minutes longer.

Add the pecan paste and stir it into the onion mixture. Whisk in the broth a little at a time, making sure each addition is well incorporated before adding more.

Add wine or water and bring to a boil, then turn down heat and simmer for 10 minutes. Salt to taste and add the cream. Simmer until warmed through. Serve with a sprinkle of nutmeg.

An elegant touch for a cold winter night.

BUTTERNUT SQUASH BISQUE

1 lg. (about 2 lbs.) butternut squash
3 golden delicious apples
3 c. chicken broth
½ c. red wine or water
½ tsp. cinnamon
½ tsp. nutmeg
¼ tsp. ground ginger
hot red pepper flakes to taste
salt and pepper to taste
3 T. fresh chopped chives (or dried chives)

Cut squash in half lengthwise and scoop out seeds. Put halves, cut side down, in a large baking dish. Peel, halve and core apples and add to pan with ¼ c. water.

Bake at 400° until squash and apples are tender, about 45 minutes. Scoop out flesh from squash and discard peels.

In a blender or food processor, blend squash, apples and broth until smooth. This can be done in batches for ease of handling. Pour into a large pot and add wine or water and seasonings. Bring to a simmer over medium high heat. Reduce heat and simmer, stirring occasionally for about 15 minutes. Salt and pepper to taste. Garnish bisque with chives.

CREAM OF ONION SOUP

1/3 c. butter or margarine
2 lbs. sweet onions, thinly
  sliced
4 cloves garlic, minced
2 c. chicken broth
1 c. white wine
1 tsp. thyme

1 bay leaf
1/2 c. each heavy cream
  and sour cream
2 T. lemon juice
salt to taste
hot sauce to taste

Melt butter or margarine over low heat and add onions.
Cover and cook until they are translucent, stirring often.
Do not let them brown. Stir in garlic, broth, wine, thyme
and bay leaf and bring to a boil. Reduce heat and simmer
until onions are soft, about 30 minutes.

Remove bay leaf and puree onions with liquid in a food
processor or blender. Then stir through a medium sieve.
Cover and chill. When ready to serve, whisk in creams,
season with lemon juice and salt and add hot sauce if
desires. Sprinkle with nutmeg for added flavor. TURN ABOUT VARIATION

FRENCH ONION SOUP
(Crockpot)

4 cans beef broth   1 meaty soup bone
2 onions, sliced   salt to taste
1/4 c. olive oil   1/4 c. white wine (optional)
1 tsp. Worcestershire sauce

Pour broth into crockpot and add soup bone. Cover and
set on high. In a large skillet, cook onions in oil
until tender. Add remaining ingredients to onions and add
to stock in crockpot. Cover and cook 6 to 8 hours on low or
3 hours on high. Remove soup bone and cut off meat and
add to soup.

Serve with a toasted round of French bread and grated
Swiss cheese.

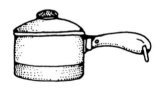

SOUTHERN CORN SOUP

1 can cream style corn
1-1/4 c. milk
dash pepper
½ c. green onions, chopped
1 tsp. honey
2 T. butter or margarine

Put corn, onions and milk in a blender or food processor and whirl for ½ minute. Add pepper and honey and blend well. Strain into a saucepan pushing as much of the soup mixture through the strainer as possible. Add butter and stir over medium heat. Garnish with chopped parsley and serve warm.

FEATHERS

NEW ORLEANS GUMBO

1 lb. pork loin, cubed
1 T. olive oil
1 T. butter or margarine
2 T. flour
1 c. beef broth
1 can stewed tomatoes
1 pkg. frozen okra (fresh can be substituted)
1 pkg. frozen succotash
hot sauce to taste
salt and pepper to taste
bay leaf

Brown pork in olive oil, 4 to 5 minutes. Remove from skillet and set aside.

Add butter to skillet and melt. Add flour and stir until roux is browned. Whisk in broth, pork and remaining ingredients. Bring to a boil. Lower heat and simmer 15 to 20 minutes. Remove bay leaf and serve.

Rice or noodles are good with this dish.

VEGETABLE RECIPES

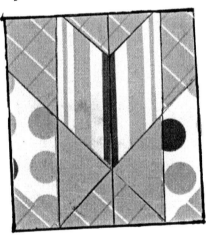

TEA LEAF

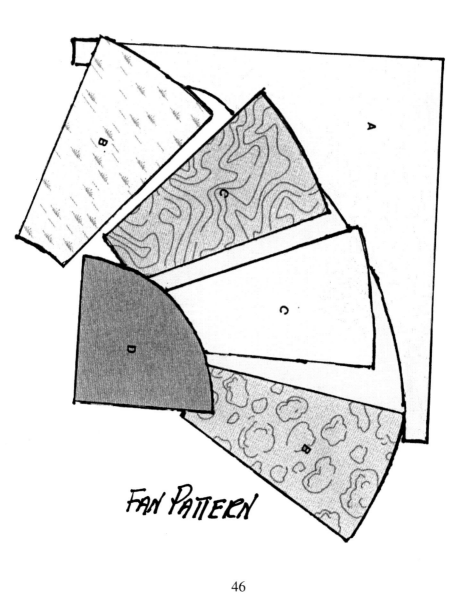

FAN PATTERN

TABLE OF CONTENTS

HAM AND COLLARD GREENS

2 qts. water
ham pieces
2 bunches collard greens, stems removed
2 c. black eyed peas (rice can be substituted)
salt and pepper to taste

Bring water to a boil and cook ham in water one hour if not cooked. If cooked, add with greens. Wash greens carefully and add to water. Add more water if necessary. Add peas or rice and heat adding salt and pepper to taste

NOTE: Other greens can be used instead of collard greens.

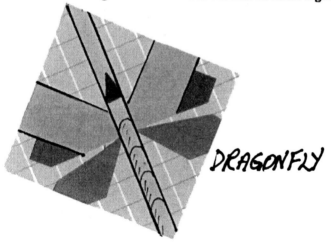

DRAGONFLY

BBQ BAKED BEANS

½ lb. bacon, diced
1 med. onion, chopped
1 15 oz. can great northern beans, drained and rinsed
1 15 oz. can black beans, drained and rinsed
¾ c. BBQ sauce
½ c. ketchup
¼ c. molasses
dash Worcestershire Sauce

Cook bacon over medium heat for about 3 minutes then add onions and cook for 5 minutes longer, until onions are soft and bacon is browned. Drain off drippings.

Add the remaining ingredients and bring to a boil. Reduce heat to low and simmer for 15 minutes longer.

TOMATOES AND OKRA CASSEROLE

1 lb. okra, fresh or frozen, sliced
1 can stewed tomatoes
1 med. onion, chopped
4 slices bacon
1 tsp. sugar

Fry bacon until crisp. Drain and crumble. Sauté onions in bacon drippings and cook until golden. Place okra in a cast iron skillet and add a little water to prevent okra from browning. Cook until smooth, adding water as necessary. Add onion, crumbled bacon, tomatoes, sugar, salt and pepper. Simmer over low heat for 15 minutes.

This is a great casserole in the summer when the okra is abundant in our gardens.

SINGING IN THE RAIN

VEGETABLE CASSEROLE

2 lg. potatoes, thinly sliced
1 lg. onion, thinly sliced
2 med. zucchini, chopped
2 carrots, thinly sliced
4 tomatoes, chopped
2 t. tarragon
salt and pepper to taste
1 c. white wine or chicken broth
3 T. butter or margarine
1 c. bread crumbs
2 c. cheddar cheese, grated

Put vegetables in casserole dish in order given and season each layer with salt, pepper and tarragon. Pour wine or broth over all, cover and bake at 375° for 1 hour.

Melt butter and stir in bread crumbs until they have absorbed the butter. Sprinkle cheese over top, then bread crumbs and bake another 15 minutes, uncovered so crumbs will brown.

Serve hot!

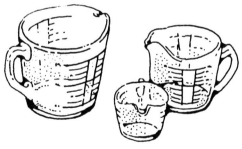

FRIED DILL PICKLES

1 c. cornmeal
2-1/4 c. flour
1 T. Worcestershire sauce
1 tsp. seasoned salt
½ tsp. pepper
¾ tsp. cayenne pepper
2 eggs, beaten
1 c. milk
½ tsp. Tabasco
¼ tsp. garlic powder
vegetable oil for frying
1 qt. dill pickles, sliced

Combine eggs, ¼ c. flour, milk, Worcestershire, Tabasco, cayenne pepper, seasoned salt and garlic powder and stir well. Set aside and combine cornmeal, balance of flour, salt and pepper and mix well.

Dip drained pickles into milk mixture and dredge in flour mixture. Deep fry at 350° until golden brown. Drain on paper towels and salt and pepper to taste.

ZUCCHINI WITH BASIL BUTTER

3 med. zucchini, sliced into ribbons
2 T. butter or margarine
1 T. olive oil
2 T. Parmesan cheese, grated
2 tsp. dried basil
1/3 tsp. red pepper flakes (or to taste)

Heat 2 T. butter or margarine in skillet and add zucchini and cook ribbons, until tender. Transfer to a bowl.

Combine remaining butter or margarine, oil, Parmesan, basil, red pepper flakes and gently toss until butter is melted. You can add a dash of garlic powder, if desired.

This is a good way to use up your zucchini crop this summer.

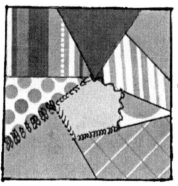

ICE CRYSTALS
CRAZY QUILT

STUFFED MUSHROOMS

5 T. chicken broth
1 c. onions, finely chopped
2 oz. cream cheese
1 10 oz. pkg. frozen spinach, chopped, squeezed dry
(or use fresh)
2 cloves garlic, minced
3 tsp. dry basil
½ c. breadcrumbs
½ c. Swiss cheese, grated
1/3 c. ricotta cheese
½ c. water chestnuts, rinsed and chopped
1/4 c. apple juice
¼ c. parsley, chopped
salt and pepper to taste
6 lg. Portabella mushrooms or button mushrooms
dry white wine

Cook onion in broth until wilted. Chop up cream cheese and stir into onion and stir until melted. Remove from heat. Stir spinach, garlic, basil, crumbs, cheeses, ricotta, chestnuts, apple juice and parsley into the onion mixture. Season with salt and pepper.

Remove stems from mushrooms and clean. Stuff each mushroom with cheese mixture and mound on top of mushroom.

Put in a pan in a single layer and pour enough white wine in the pan to cover bottom and bake at 400° for 10 minutes. *This is great as an appetizer or a vegetable side dish.*

GRILLED PORTABELLA SANDWICH

2 lg. portabella mushrooms
1 T. each mayonnaise and sour cream
½ tsp. lemon juice
1 tsp. olive oil
2 crusty rolls, halved
1 clove garlic
2 T. dried basil
1 tomato, sliced

Combine mayonnaise, sour cream and lemon juice and mix well. Brush mushrooms with oil and grill until tender. Toast rolls on grill and rub with garlic clove.

Spread mayonnaise mixture on roll halves and top with mushroom, sliced tomato and basil. Serve immediately.

This is a great summertime sandwich that's quick, very easy and oh so tasty!

BAKED ONIONS WITH RAISINS AND PECANS

4 sweet onions	1/2 c. bread crumbs
1/4 c. clarified butter	1 T. seasoned salt
1/2 c. raisins, soaked in	1 T. sugar
warm water to plump	1/2 c. pecans. chopped
1 T. sugar	1/2 c. chicken broth

Cut onions in half. Place 8 onion halves into a lightly greased, deep pan and sprinkle with raisins, pecans, bread crumbs, salt and sugar. Drizzle with butter and pour chicken broth into pan. Cover with foil and roast in a 375° oven for 30-40 minutes, until tender.

WIND MILL

VEGETABLE CASSEROLE II

2 T. butter or margarine   1 med. green pepper, cubed
1 med. eggplant, peeled and 2 tsp. dill
    sliced in 1/2" slices   1/2 T. Italian seasoning
2 med. zucchini, in 1/2 slices 1/2 c. each Swiss cheese and
2 lg. sweet onions, sliced   Cheddar, grated
2 lg. tomatoes, sliced   salt and pepper to taste
Melt butter or margarine and pour into baking pan. Layer
vegetable and sprinkle on seasonings and cheeses. Cover
and bake at 350° for 30 to 35 minutes until hot and cheeses
are melted.

MARINATED BAKED SWEET ONIONS

4 lg. sweet onions, cut in
   1/2" slices
1/2 c. white wine vinegar
1 tsp. basil
1 tsp. thyme
1 tsp. oregano

1/2 tsp. sugar
salt and pepper to taste
1 c. salad oil
parsley
paprika

Arrange onion slices in a single layer on a baking sheet.
Combine oil, vinegar, basil, thyme, oregano, sugar, salt
and pepper and mix well. Pour over onions and marinate
at room temperature for up to 2 hours. Pour off and
reserve marinade and bake onions, covered, at 325° for 30
minutes. Uncover and baste with marinade and sprinkle
with paprika. Continue baking for 45 minutes to 1 hour
longer or until onions are tender. Garnish with parsley.

SWEET ONION & SUMMER VEGETABLES MEDLEY

1 tsp. olive oil
1 tsp. minced garlic
1 sweet onion, thinly
   sliced lengthwise into
   slivers

3 ears corn, cut from the
   cob
1/2 lb. baby zucchini, cut
   into 1/4" rounds
salt and pepper to taste

Heat oil over medium heat and add garlic and onion, sauté until transparent, about 5 minutes. Add corn, zucchini and 1/4 to 1/2 c. water and cook, stirring occasionally, until tender and caramelized, 10 minutes. Season with salt and pepper. Serve on warmed tortillas or crusty bread.

LADY BUG

SCALLOPED SWEET ONIONS

3 lg. sweet onions, peeled and sliced
½ tsp. salt
¼ c. butter or margarine
1 c. milk
2 c. cheddar cheese, grated

Slice onions and separate into rings. Place in a1-1/2 qt.
casserole. Melt butter and blend in flour. Slowly stir in
milk and cook until thickened, stirring continuously. Stir
in salt and cheese. Pour over onions.

Bake uncovered for 1 hour at 375°.

SWEET POTATO CASSEROLE

3 c. cooked sweet potatoes
1 c. sugar
2 eggs
½ c. milk
½ c. butter or margarine, melted
1/ tsp. vanilla
1 tsp. cinnamon
1 tsp. nutmeg

Topping:
1 c. brown sugar
1/3 c. flour
1/3 c. butter or margarine, melted
½ c. pecans, chopped

Combine potatoes, sugar, eggs, milk and butter. Stir in vanilla and spices. Put into a greased casserole.

Mix topping ingredients together and sprinkle on top of potato mixture. Bake at 350° for 30 minutes or until top is brown.

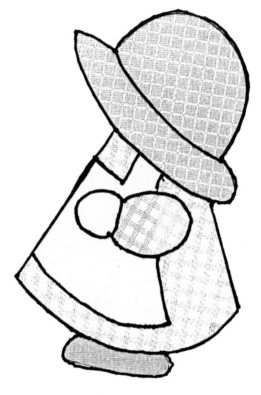

SUN BONNET SUE

LOG CABIN

SALAD RECIPES

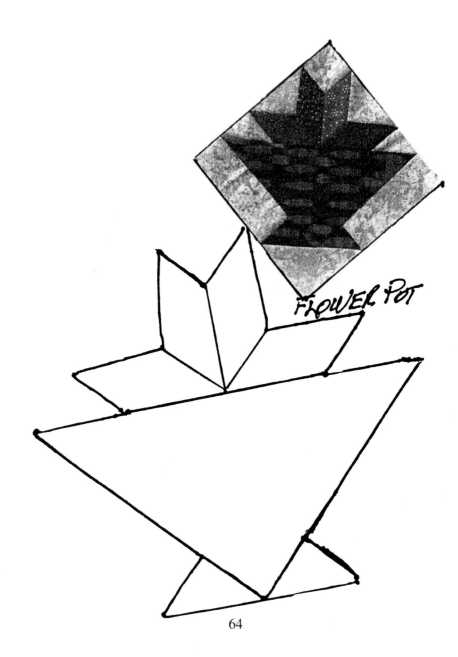

FLOWER POT

64

TABLE OF CONTENTS

SWEET TATER SALAD

2 c. sweet potatoes, cooked and cubed
1 small onion, chopped
1/2c. celery, chopped
1 T. oil
2 tsp. vinegar
salt and pepper to taste

Combine all ingredients and mix well. Chill for several hours and serve.

This salad can be made ahead of time and left to chill until ready to serve. Great for a quick summer supper.

PECAN CHICKEN SALAD

1 c. chicken, cooked and chopped
1 c. rice, cooked
½ c. grapes (red or green), halved
½ c. mayonnaise
2 T. red onions, minced
2 T. dried basil
salt and pepper to taste
¼ c. pecans, chopped

Combine all ingredients except pecans and chill thoroughly. Serve on a lettuce leaf and sprinkle with pecans.

DIAMOND LILY

PINEAPPLE PECAN CHICKEN SALAD

2 c. chicken, cooked
1 c. pineapple chunks,
drained
2/3 c. mayonnaise
½ c. celery, diced
½ c. pecans, chopped
¼ c. red bell pepper, diced
2 T. dried basil

Heat chicken and pineapple in top of a double boiler.
Add mayonnaise and mix lightly. Warm about 5
minutes more.

Stir in celery and pecans. Stir until warmed through.
Spoon into a serving dish and sprinkle with additional
pecans, bell pepper and basil.

PASTA CHICKEN SALAD

1 sm. red onion, chopped
1 lb. sm. pasta shells etc.
1 lg. chicken breast, cooked
½ c. peas, fresh or frozen
salt and pepper to taste
½ c. mayonnaise

Cook pasta according to package directions. Cook fresh peas until tender, or microwave frozen peas for about 2 minutes. Let pasta and peas cool while slicing chicken breast into slivers. Toss chicken with onion, pasta and peas. Season with salt and pepper and add enough mayonnaise until all ingredients are combines. Serve immediately.

TOMATO PIE

1 9 inch pie shell, partially baked
1 T. olive oil
2 T. dried basil
1 T. garlic, minced
8 oz. mozzarella, thinly sliced
8 roma tomatoes, seeded and thinly sliced
½ c. Parmesan or Asiago cheese, grated

Bake shell 10 minutes at 375° until light brown. In a small saucepan heat oil and garlic just until heated through. Arrange half of the mozzarella on bottom of partially baked crust, sprinkle with half the basil and layer half of the tomatoes. Sprinkle with Parmesan or Asiago. Repeat layers. Spoon garlic and oil mixture pie and bake at 375° for 15 minutes or until cheese is melted and crust is golden brown. Let stand 5 minutes before cutting.

This is great in the summer when the tomatoes are fresh from the garden.

CHICKEN SALAD

1 c. chicken, cooked
1 c. rice, cooked
½ c. grapes, halved
½ c. mayonnaise
2 T. basil, dried
ground pepper
¼ c. pecans, chopped

Combine all ingredients and chill until ready to serve.

JICAMA SLAW

1 sm. jicama*   2 tsp. Dijon mustard
1 T. white wine vinegar
1 carrot   1/4 c. red onion, thinly sliced
2 T. olive oil

Peel jicama and carrot and shred finely in a food processor.
Separate onion into rings. Combine vinegar, mustard and
oil and whisk until blended. Add vegetables, and salt and
pepper to taste and toss.

*Jicama can be found in Hispanic markets or in specialty
produce markets.

TOMATO AND ONION SALAD

1 lb. sweet onions
1 lg. tomato, cored and cut
   into 1/4" slices

fresh basil for garnish
salt and pepper to taste

Dressing:
1/4 c. olive oil
3 T. red wine vinegar
2 T. pesto sauce

Slice the onions thinly and separate into rings. Put in a
bowl and pour dressing over them, toss to coat.

To make dressing, whisk all ingredients together.

On 4 plates, arrange equal portions of the tomato and top
with portions of the onions and dressing. Garnish with
basil and season with salt and pepper.

SWEET ONION, CHICKEN AND APPLE SALAD

3 c. apples, unpeeled and
   diced
2 c. chicken, cooked and
   diced
1 c. sweet onion, chopped

1/4 c. golden raisins
1/4 c. pecans, chopped
1 c. celery, sliced
dressing, recipe follows

In a large bowl, combine apples, chicken, onions, celery, raisins and pecans. Top with Creamy Apple dressing and toss to coat. Serve immediately or cover and refrigerate until ready to serve.

Apple Yogurt Dressing
1/2 cup plain yogurt
1/3 c. mayonnaise
1/4 c. frozen apple juice,
   thawed

1 T. lemon juice
dash salt and pepper

In a small bowl combine all ingredients and mix well.

ONION SALAD

1 c. onions, finely chopped
¾ c. stuffed green olives, finely chopped
2 T. capers, drained
2 cloves garlic, minced
¾ c. celery, finely chopped
2 T. oregano, dried
¼ c. olive oil
1 T. balsamic vinegar

Mix all ingredients together and store, covered, in the refrigerator.

This is great on crusty French bread with sandwich meats and cheeses of your choice.

If Vidalia or other sweet onions are available, use them. They are wonderful in this salad.

SWEET & SOUR ONIONS AND CUCUMBERS

3 c. cucumbers, thinly sliced 1/4 c. sugar
   and seeded   2 T. fresh dill, chopped
1-1/2 c. sweet onions, thinly 1/2 c. carrot, grated
   sliced   1/2 c. vinegar
salt and pepper to taste

In a bowl, combine cucumbers, onions and carrots and set aside. Combine vinegar, sugar, dill, 2 T. water, salt and pepper. Pour over cucumber and onions and toss. Serve immediately or refrigerate until ready to serve.

OVERALL ANDY

PASTA AND RICE RECIPES

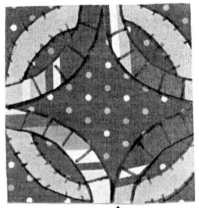

DOUBLE WEDDING
RING

MARINER'S COMPASS

TABLE OF CONTENTS

DIRTY RICE DRESSING

1 lb. ground beef
1 c. uncooked rice
1 can cream of onion soup
1 can cream of chicken soup
3 green onions, chopped
1 green bell pepper, chopped
½ tsp. garlic, minced
½ tsp. Cajun seasoning (or more to taste)
2 T. oil
salt and pepper to taste

Lightly brown ground beef in oil and add remaining ingredients and mix well. Put into a casserole dish and back at 300° for 40 minutes or until rice is tender.

A great potluck dish and very tasty too!

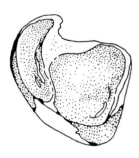

GRITS AND CHEESE CASSEROLE

4 c. milk
1 c. grits (any brand)
½ c. butter or margarine
2 eggs, beaten
½ tsp. baking powder
¼ tsp. salt
1 c. cheddar cheese, grated

Bring 3-1/2 c. milk to a boil and gradually stir in grits.
Cook over medium heat, stirring constantly, until thick.
Remove from heat and stir in eggs, baking powder, salt and
remaining milk.

Pour into a 2 qt. casserole and bake uncovered 30 minutes.
Sprinkle grated cheese over top and bake 15 additional
minutes.

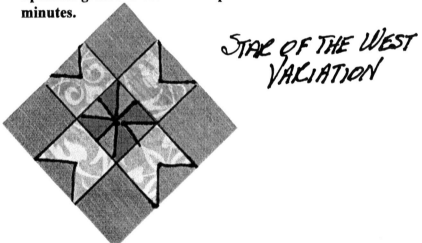

STAR OF THE WEST
VARIATION

EGGPLANT PASTA

1 eggplant, diced
2 T. salt
¼ c. olive oil
2 c. spaghetti sauce of choice
¼ c. basil, chopped
1 c. red wine or apple juice
½ lb. pasta, cooked

Mix the salt with the diced eggplant and let sit in a colander for 30 minutes. Rinse and pat dry.

In a large skillet, sauté eggplant until browned. Combine spaghetti sauce, basil and wine or juice and mix into the eggplant. When eggplant is tender, remove from heat. Salt and pepper to taste. Pour over cooked pasta and sprinkle with grated Romano or Parmesan cheese.

KAREN'S BREAD STUFFING

½ lb. bacon, cut into ½ inch pieces, cooked
2 c. onion, chopped
1-1/2 c. celery, chopped
1-1/2 c. carrots, chopped
1 T. fresh thyme, chopped
1 tsp. caraway seeds
salt and pepper to taste
½ c. red wine or chicken broth
2 c. tart apples, chopped
8 c. rye bread cubes, toasted or dried
1 lb. fresh sauerkraut, rinsed well and drained

Using 4 T. bacon drippings, cook onion, celery, carrots, thyme, caraway seeds, salt and pepper. Cook until vegetables soften, about 10 minutes. Add wine or broth and bring to a boil, scraping pan to loosen browned bits on bottom.

Add apples, cover and cook until apples are tender. Remove from heat and stir in cooked bacon. In a large bowl, pour over bread cubes and sauerkraut. Toss to combine.

You can use this to stuff a chicken or turkey or bake as a casserole. If using as a casserole, pour a cup of chicken broth over cubes. Bake covered for 45 minutes to 1 hour. Uncover and let top crisp the last 15 minutes.

ARKANSAS SPAGHETTI BAKE

1 12 oz. pkg. spaghetti or angel hair pasta
1-1/2 lb. ground beef
2 c. tomatoes, diced
1 jar prepared spaghetti sauce
1 c. water
1 c. white wine or chicken broth
1-1/2 tsp. sugar
1-1/2 tsp. oregano
1 c. Parmesan cheese, grated
½ lb. mozzarella, sliced
½ c. red bell pepper, diced
4 cloves garlic, minced
½ c. fresh parsley, chopped
salt and pepper to taste

Cook pasta per package instructions. Crumble ground beef in a skillet and cook until browned. Set aside.

In a large saucepan, combine tomatoes, spaghetti sauce, water, wine or broth, onion, garlic, parsley, oregano, sugar and bay leaves. Bring to a boil and simmer, covered for 1 hour. Remove bay leaves. Reserve 1 cup sauce for later. Add cooked beef to sauce and simmer for 20 minutes.

(more)

(con't)

Cover bottom of a 9 x 13 inch baking dish with a thin layer
of sauce. Then alternate layers of pasta, Parmesan cheese
and sauce. The last layer should be sauce. Cover with foil
and bake at 350° for 30 minutes. Uncover and lay slices of
mozzarella on top and cook, uncovered, for 5 minutes or
until cheese melts.

Allow to cool for about 15 minutes, this will make it easier
to slice. Cut into squares and surround with a small pool of
reserved sauce. Sprinkle with grated Parmesan.

ARTICHOKE FETTUCCINI WITH BASIL

8 oz. fettuccini, cooked
2 9 oz. pkgs. artichoke hearts, thawed
2 T. Parmesan cheese
2 red bell peppers, seeded
and chopped
½ onion, chopped
2 cloves, garlic, minced
1 T. olive oil
1 tomato, chopped
3 T. dried basil
2 T. Parmesan cheese
1 c. spinach
¼ c. sherry
¼ c. chicken broth

Heat olive oil in a large skillet over medium high heat. Add artichokes and pepper and sauté 3 minutes. Add onion, garlic, tomato and basil and sauté another 2 minutes. Add sherry and bring to a boil for 2 minutes. Add spinach and Parmesan. Mix until heated through and spinach begins to wilt. Add broth and bring to a boil. Cover and simmer until heated. Serve over the fettuccini.

QUICHE

1 pastry shell
2 T. butter or margarine
3 green onions, chopped
3 eggs
¾ c. Cheddar cheese, grated
¼ c. chicken broth
2 T. basil, dried
½ c. parsley, chopped
salt and pepper to taste
2 T. Parmesan cheese

Bake pastry shell about 15 minutes until lightly browned.

Melt butter or margarine in saucepan and add green
onions, cook about 2 minutes. Combine eggs, cream, and
cheese in bowl and add onions. Pour into shell. Peel
tomatoes and cut into thin slices. Roll tomato slices in basil
and Parmesan mixture and place on top of leek mixture.
Sprinkle with salt, pepper and Parmesan.

Bake at 350° for about 30 minutes or until center is set.

NOT YOUR ORDINARY MAC AND CHEESE

2 c. macaroni, cooked
2 c. Cheddar cheese, grated
1 c. Swiss cheese, grated
1 c. heavy cream
2 eggs
2 T. butter or margarine
salt and pepper to taste
2 tomatoes, sliced
dry basil leaves, crumbled
½ c. Cheddar cheese, grated (for topping)

Combine cheeses, salt, pepper, cream and eggs and mix well. Stir in macaroni and spread half of this mixture in a greased casserole dish. Arrange basil and tomatoes over layer and top with remaining macaroni. Melt butter or margarine and cook the breadcrumbs until golden. Combine crumbs and ½ c. cheese and sprinkle over top. Bake at 200° until topping is a golden brown. *Great as a side dish or a meal on its' own.*

TUNA PASTA SALAD WITH BASIL DRESSING

¼ c. dried basil, crumbled fine
1 c. sour cream
1 tsp. lemon juice
salt and pepper to taste
½ c. half & half
1 can albacore tuna
12 oz. bow tie pasta, cooked

In food processor or blender, combine all ingredients except tuna and pasta and blend well. Add tuna and stir gently into pasta until coated with dressing. Garnish with a basil leaf and chill.

DRESDEN PLATE

PASTA WITH MUSHROOM SAUCE

2 T. butter or margarine
¼ c. olive oil
1 lb. Portobello mushrooms
2 cloves garlic, mashed
¼ tsp. red pepper flakes
1 c. chicken broth
½ c. white wine or water
1 chicken bouillon cube
1-1/2 T. parsley
salt and pepper to taste
1` lb. tubular pasta of choice
¼ c. Parmesan cheese, grated

Chop mushrooms into small pieces. Combine butter and oil in a large skillet and sauté mushrooms. Add garlic and red pepper flakes. Cook over medium heat until liquid from the mushrooms evaporates, about 10 minutes.

Add broth, wine or water and bouillon cube and increase heat to high cooking 10 minutes to blend and for the liquid to reduce somewhat. Remove from heat and add salt, pepper and parsley.

Cook pasta according to package directions and drain completely. Return to pot and add mushroom sauce and stir over medium heat until warmed. Remove from heat and add Parmesan cheese. Toss to mix.

STEW RECIPES

STREAK OF LIGHTNING

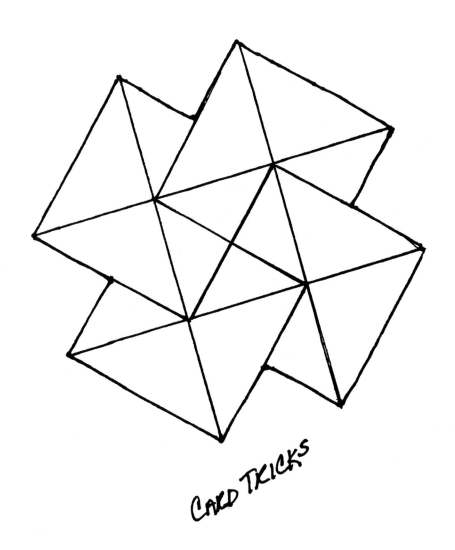

CARD TRICKS

TABLE OF CONTENTS

WINTER STEW

3 lbs. beef round, cut into
   cubes
2 T. olive oil
salt and pepper to taste
1 c. beef broth
1 c. tomato sauce

2 med. zucchini, halved and
   cut crosswise into 1" pcs.
1 15 oz. can black beans,
   drained
½ c. fresh corn kernels
2 T. cornstarch

In a heavy skillet, heat oil and cook beef over medium heat until browned. Season with salt and pepper. Stir in broth and tomato sauce and bring to a boil. Reduce heat to low and cover and simmer for 1-1/2 hours.

Stir in vegetables and bring to a boil again. Reduce heat, cover and simmer for another 20 minutes, until tender but not overcooked. Mix cornstarch with water and stir into mixture. Cook until thickened.

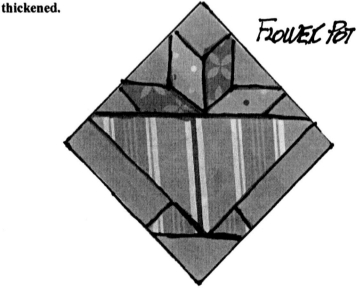

FLOWER POT

APPLE CIDER STEW

2 lbs. beef stew meat
2 T. olive oil
¼ c. flour
2 c. water
1 c. apple cider
½ c. steak sauce
2 tsp. thyme
salt and pepper to taste
1 bay leaf
3 medium potatoes, peeled and cubed
3 carrots, sliced
1 onion, chopped
1 c. fresh green beans (frozen can be substituted)

Over high heat, brown beef in olive oil. Stir in flour.
Slowly stir in water, cider and steak sauce. Bring to a boil
and stir in thyme, salt, pepper and bay leaf. Reduce heat,
cover and simmer for 2 hours.

Add potatoes, onion and beans. Cover and cook an
additional 30 minutes or until vegetables are tender.
Remove bay leaf before serving.

This is good served with browned noodles or rice.

GREEN CHILE LAMB STEW

1 lb. lean lamb, cubed
1 onion, chopped
6 cloves garlic, minced
2 cans (15 oz. each) whole tomatoes, undrained
1 lb. potatoes, peeled
3 cans (4 oz. each) diced mild green chiles
1 tsp oregano
1 med. zucchini, chopped
1 c. corn kernels (frozen can be substituted)

Combine ½ c. water, lamb, onion and garlic in a large saucepan and bring to a simmer. Cover and continue simmering about 30 minutes or until onion is tender. Increase heat, uncover and boil, stirring occasionally until liquid evaporates and browns. Add tomatoes and liquid. Cover and simmer for another 30 minutes.

Chop potatoes in 1 inch cubes and add with chiles and oregano. Cover and continue cooking until potatoes and lamb are tender, about 30 minutes.

SWEET & SOUR BEEF STEW

1-1/2 lbs. beef stew meat, cubed
2 T. olive oil
2 carrots, shredded
2 med. onions, sliced thinly
1 8 oz. can tomato sauce
1 c. *Syrah*
¼ c. brown sugar
¼ c. cider vinegar
1 T. Worcestershire sauce
¼ c. chives, chopped
salt and pepper to taste
2 tsp. cornstarch
2 T. cold water

In a large skillet, brown half the beef at a time in the oil. Return all meat to pan and stir in other ingredients, except water and cornstarch.

Cover and cook over low heat about 1-1/2 hours or until meat is tender. Combine cornstarch and water and add to stew, stirring occasionally until it boils. Turn to simmer and let thicken.

Serve with hot buttered noodles and crispy French bread.

BEEF STEW WITH WINE

3 lbs. beef chuck, cut into large pieces
1 lg. onion, finely chopped
2 carrots, finely chopped
2 cloves garlic, peeled
Bouquet Garni (see below)
1 bottle red wine
6 oz. lean salt pork, diced
salt and pepper to taste
1/3 c. flour
1 lb. small white mushrooms, stems trimmed

Combine beef, onions, carrots, garlic and bouquet garni into a large bowl and add wine. Using your hands, mix all ingredients together. Cover bowl and refrigerate for 24 hours.

Remove beef from marinade, reserving marinade, and dry meat well. Fry salt pork in a large pot over medium heat until crisp, about 7 or 8 minutes. Season beef with salt and pepper. Add to pot and brown on all sides. Sprinkle in flour and cook, stirring constantly, for 3 minutes, Add marinade and 2 c. water and bring to a boil over high heat, scraping up browned bits from pan. Reduce heat to low, cover and cook about 3 hours or until meat is tender. Add mushrooms and cook 30 additional minutes. Remove bouquet garni before serving.

(more)

(con't)

TRADITIONAL BOUQUET GARNI:
3 stalks parsley
1 sprig thyme
1 bay leaf

Tie together with twine so it can be removed easily. You can add
your own choice of herbs.

SUN BONNET SUE

VENISON STEW

1 lb. ground venison (ground beef may be substituted)
2 cans Rotel tomatoes
1 tsp. sugar
2 tsp. salt
1 beef bouillon cube
2 med. onions, chopped
½ lb. carrots, chopped
4 lg. potatoes, unpeeled and diced
½ bunch celery, chopped
2 cloves garlic, minced

Brown venison or beef in a heavy skillet. Do not drain. Add additional olive oil if too dry. Add remaining ingredients, cover and simmer for 4 hours. Add water if necessary.

Ground venison is exceptional in this recipe, if you can get it. It has a wilder and more distinct flavor than the ground beef.

GARBANZO STEW

2 lbs. dried garbanzo beans
1 onion, chopped
10 c. water
4 lbs. stew meat (venison can be substituted), cut into
cubes
salt and pepper to taste

Soak beans overnight. Drain and rinse under cold
water. Put into a large pot with water and boil over
high heat. Reduce heat to low and simmer uncovered,
about 2-1/2 hours, stirring occasionally, adding
additional water if necessary.

Brown meat in olive oil and add with balance of
ingredients to beans. Cook another 2 hours or until
meat is tender and the beans are cooked.

NEW MEXICO BLACK BEAN CHILI

1 c. beef, cut into cubes (pork or turkey can be substituted)
2 Cans black beans, drained
1 bell pepper, seeded and chopped
1 can diced tomatoes, undrained
1 sm. red onion, sliced
1 can chopped green chiles (more if desired)
½ T. cumin
2 tsp. chile powder
1 clove garlic
salt to taste
2 cans tomato sauce (more if desired)
½ c. sour cream
2 T. cilantro

Put all ingredients into crock-pot except sour cream and cilantro. Cover and cook 8 to 9 hours on low (4 to 5 hours on high).

Serve with sour cream and cilantro on top.

ROUNDHOUSE STEW

2 lbs. beef shanks
8 c. water
1 T. salt
2 onions, chopped
peppercorns to taste
4 potatoes diced
6 carrots, chopped
4 stalks celery, chopped
basil leaves
¼ tsp. thyme
bay leaf

Combine meat, water, bay leaf, salt and peppercorns and bring to a boil. Skim off top. Simmer 3 hours covered.. Remove bay leaf and add vegetables and herbs. Cook ½ hour longer or until vegetables are tender.

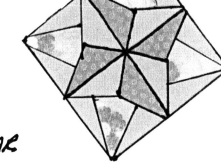

8 POINT STAR

SUN BONNET SUE

BEEF, PORK AND LAMB RECIPES

SEE SAW

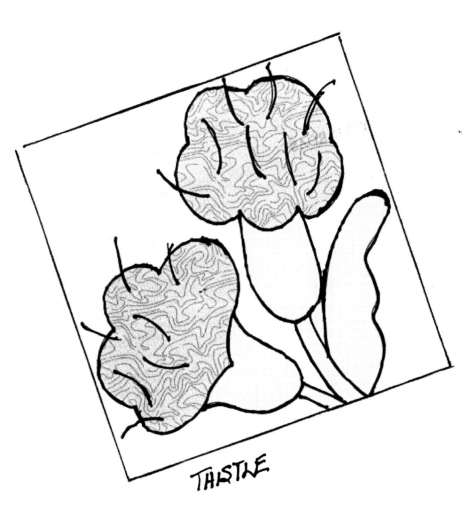

THISTLE

106

TABLE OF CONTENTS

EYE-OF-ROUND STEAK WITH EGGPLANT SAUTÈ

3 T. olive oil, divided
8 to 10 sm. eggplants, chopped into ½ inch cubes
4 ripe tomatoes, cut into large chunks
1 green bell pepper, cut into 1-inch pieces
12 pitted kalamata
olives, quartered
2 T. basil, minced
2 T. thyme, minced
2 T. oregano, minced
salt and pepper to taste
4 eye-of-round steaks
½ c. red wine or apple juice

Heat 2 T. oil in a large skillet over medium high heat. Add eggplant and cook stirring often until soft, about 15 minutes. Add tomatoes, stirring until they give up their juice, about 5 minutes. Add peppers; cook 2 minutes. Stir in olives, basil, thyme, oregano, salt and pepper, cook 2 to 3 minutes longer.

Heat remaining oil in a large cast iron skillet, and cook steaks 2 at a time. Just cook until browned. Repeat with remaining steaks.

Remove steaks and add wine. Cook 1 minute, scraping up brown bits from the bottom of the pan. Spoon sauce over steaks and serve with remaining sauce. Top steaks with vegetable mixture.

LAMB AND PRUNES

Olive oil
2 lbs. breast of lamb, cut into serving size pieces
2 tsp. seasoned salt
pepper to taste
2 cloves garlic, sliced
1 can tomato paste
1 T. thyme
1 c. red wine or water
2 onions, sliced
3 carrots, sliced
1 c. dried prunes

Brown lamb in a small amount of oil. Season meat with salt and pepper.

Add garlic, tomato paste, thyme and wine or water. Cover pan and simmer for 45 minutes. Add onions, carrots, prunes and 1 c. water to meat. Cover and simmer another 45 minutes or until vegetables are tender. Add more wine at this point if you wish.

Serve with wild or plain rice.

Don't let the prunes throw you off track. They add a wonderful flavor.

BOEUF
BOURGUIGNON ala CROCKPOT

1 14 oz. can beef broth
1 c. red wine or water
¼ c. water
1 pkg. plain brown gravy mix
2 tsp. garlic, minced
2 bay leaves
¾ tsp. thyme
5 slices, ready-cooked bacon
1 lg. onion, chopped
20 baby carrots
8 oz. fresh mushrooms, sliced
2 lbs. beef cubes
1 bag (16 oz.) frozen sm. onions
salt and pepper to taste
3 T. cornstarch

Combine beef broth, wine and water into crock-pot. Add powdered gravy and whisk until lumps disappear. Add garlic, bay leaves and thyme.

Cut bacon into ¼ inch pieces and scatter in pot. Add chopped onion, carrots and mushrooms. Place beef cubes evenly on top of vegetables and press down. Stir to submerge beef in liquid. Add whole onions to pot. Cover and cook on low setting for 8-9 hours. When finished cooking remove lid and stir well. Remove bay leaves and season with salt and pepper.

(more)

(con't)
Combine cornstarch and 3 T. water and whisk until
smooth. Pour evenly over stew and stir well. Continue
stirring until stew reaches desired thickness, about 5
minutes. Serve in bowls with crusty bread for dipping.

*This is a great meal to eat in front of the fireplace on a cold
winter night.*

LOG CABIN

HAM STEAK IN PINOT NOIR

2 ham slices, about ¾ inch thick
1 c. sweet cider
1 c. water
½ c. maple syrup
¾ c. cranberries
¾ c. golden raisins
6 slices pineapple (optional)
4 cloves
juice of 1 orange

Put ham in crock pot (roll if necessary to fit). Add remaining ingredients. Cover and cook on high for 1 hour. Reduce heat to low for about 6 hours.

Remove ham slices and thicken gravy. Turn crock-pot to high and combine cornstarch with water and stir into sauce until thickened.

Serve slices with sauce over them and also serve some on the side.

SYRAH BRAISED LAMB SHANKS

4 lamb shanks, trimmed
salt and pepper to taste
2 T. olive oil, add more if necessary
2 med. onions, diced
2 celery stalks, diced
2 carrots, diced
2 c. red wine or water
1 c. beef broth
3 cloves garlic, crushed
2 bay leaves

In an ovenproof pan, season shanks with salt and pepper and brown in olive oil, about 5 minutes. Transfer to a plate and add vegetables to the pan. Cook until they are golden brown. Remove pan from heat and add wine. Return to medium high heat and simmer. Scrape browned bits from bottom of pan.

Add broth, garlic, bay leaves and shanks and bring to a boil. Cover the pan and put in the oven and bake at 350° for about 2 hours. The meat should be falling off the bones.

Transfer meat to a large serving bowl and remove bay leaves. Using a stick blender puree liquids in pan until smooth. Pour some of the sauce over the shanks and serve the rest on the side.

QUICK AND EASY CROCKPOT PORK ROAST

4 lb. boneless pork roast
1-1/2 c. water
1 c. white wine or apple juice
salt and pepper to taste
1 tsp. thyme
1 tsp. sage, ground
1 clove garlic, minced

Put roast in the crock-pot. Combine all other ingredients and pour over roast. Cover and cook on low 5 to 6 hours.

This is an easy dinner that you can put on before you leave for work and it will be ready when you get home.
Serve with rice and a green salad and your meal is ready.

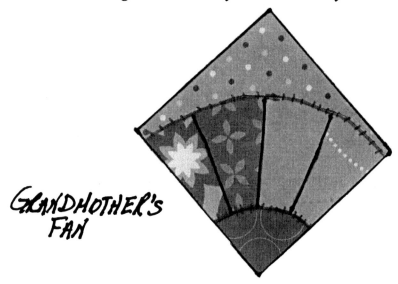

GRANDMOTHER'S
FAN

SWISS STEAK

1-1/2 lbs. sirloin or round steak about 1-1/2 inch thick
flour
salt and pepper to taste
chile powder to taste
3 T. olive oil
2 onions, sliced
1 lb. tomatoes, chopped (or substitute 1 lg. can diced
tomatoes)
½ tsp. thyme
1 c. water0

Combine flour, chile powder, salt and pepper and dredge steak. Brown in olive oil and remove from skillet. Add onions and sauté until soft and golden. Return meat to pan and add tomatoes, thyme and water.

Cover and simmer for about 1-1/2 to 2 hours or until meat is tender. Turn the meat occasionally. More wine can be added to thin the gravy.

CINNAMON
PINEAPPLE PORK TENDERLOIN

1 lb. pork tenderloin, cut into 8 pieces crosswise
½ tsp. salt
2 T. butter or margarine, divided
1 red bell pepper, julienne
1 8 oz. can pineapple chunks in natural juice, undrained
½ c. white wine or water
1 T. ginger root, finely chopped
1 jalapeño pepper, finely chopped
1/8 tsp. cinnamon
1 T. fresh cilantro, chopped

Pound each tenderloin piece to about a 1-inch thickness.
Sprinkle with salt. Add 1 T. butter to a skillet until melted
and cook each tenderloin until browned, about 3 minutes a
side. Remove to a platter and keep warm.

Melt the remaining butter and sauté bell pepper quickly,
about 3 minutes. Reduce heat to low and add pineapple
and juice, wine or water, ginger, jalapeño and cinnamon.
Simmer gently until reduced to about ¼ c.

Turn off heat and return medallions of pork to coat in
sauce. Serve with any remaining sauce on top. Sprinkle
with cilantro.

GLAZED PORK CHOPS

2 T. olive oil

4 pork chops, 1/3" thick
1 lg. onion, thinly sliced
¼ c. Worcestershire sauce
¼ c. water
1 T. brown sugar
¼ tsp. sage

Season chops and sauté in oil until almost done, about 8 minutes, turning once. Remove from skillet and add onion to pan and cook until golden brown, about 6 minutes.

Stir in Worcestershire sauce, water, brown sugar and sage; bring to a boil. Lower heat and continue cooking until slightly reduced and thickened.

Return chops to pan and simmer uncovered about 2 minutes or until chops are done and glazed.

ITALIAN SAUSAGE AND CHICKEN WITH OLIVES

4 Italian sausages, sweet or hot
2 T. olive oil
3 cloves garlic, finely minced
6 chicken breasts, skinless and boneless
salt and pepper to taste
½ c. water
1 each red and green bell peppers, sliced in strips
1 c. fresh mushrooms, sliced
1 sweet onion, chopped (Vidalia is good, if they are in season)
¼ c. oregano, chopped
2 T. fresh tarragon, chopped
½ c. black olives, chopped

Cut sausage into bite-size pieces and brown in olive oil, and remove from pan. Add garlic and sauté about 2 minutes, being careful not to burn. Salt and pepper chicken and sauté with garlic about 5 minutes a side or until no longer pink in the middle. Remove and keep warm.

Add water to skillet and scrap up browned bits. Heat about 2 minutes then add sausage, chicken, peppers, mushroom and onions. Stir in oregano, tarragon, salt, pepper and olives. Cover and simmer 20 minutes until chicken is tender.

Serve with hot buttered noodles or rice.

BRISKET BRAISED IN WINE

1 T. olive oil
2 lbs. beef brisket (I prefer the flat cut)
salt and pepper to taste
1 c. red wine or water
1 med. onion, diced
4 cloves garlic, minced
2 med. tomatoes, chopped (substitute 1 can diced tomatoes)
4 carrots, peeled
4 stalks celery
½ c. chicken broth
¼ c. water
1 tsp. thyme, chopped
1 tsp. rosemary, chopped
1 bay leaf

Season brisket with salt and pepper and, in an ovenproof skillet, sear in olive oil over high heat. Remove brisket and add wine or water. Scrape bottom of pan to loosen browned bits and reduce wine for 2 minutes. Add garlic and cook for 1 additional minute.

Return brisket to pan and add remaining ingredients and bring to a simmer. Remove pan from heat and cover. Place in oven at 250° and cook for 2-1/2 to 3 hours, or until meat is tender.

Remove brisket and slice against the grain in thin slices. Arrange in a baking dish and cover with sauce.

AUSTRIALIAN STYLE BARBEQUE MEATLOAF

Meatloaf:
1 lb. ground beef
1 lb. sausage, casings removed
1 c. fine breadcrumbs
2 med. onions, chopped fine
1 T. curry powder
½ c. water
1 T. parsley, chopped
1 egg, beaten
1 clove garlic, minced
½ c. milk
salt and pepper to taste

Sauce:
1 onion, chopped fine
¼ c. water
½ c. catsup
¼ c. red wine
¼ c. Worcestershire sauce
2 T. cider vinegar
1 T. instant coffee
¼ brown sugar, firmly packed
1 oz. butter or margarine
2 tsp. lemon juice

(more)

(con't)
For the meatloaf, combine meats, breadcrumbs, onions, salt, pepper, garlic, parsley, curry and egg in a large bowl. Mix well. Combine water and milk and add to meat mixture a little at a time until firm. Shape into loaf and put into a greased baking pan. Bake 30 minutes at 375°.

For the sauce, sauté onions in butter until golden and add all other ingredients. Bring to a boil, then lower heat and simmer 10 to 15 minutes. After loaf has cooked for 30 minutes, pour half of the sauce over the meat,. Return loaf to oven and bake an additional 45 minutes. Baste often with remaining sauce.

When cooled enough to slice, cut thick slices and serve with remaining sauce.

This sauce is also good with ribs, chicken or pork chops.

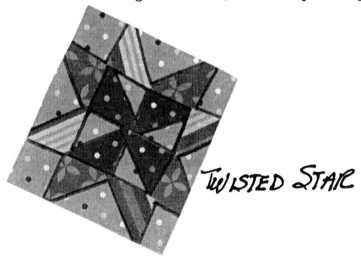

TWISTED STAR

CARNE GUISADA

(Stewed beef)

1 lg. rump roast, trimmed and cut into 1" cubes
2 T. olive oil
2 c. water
2 med. potatoes, peeled and cut into 1" pieces
1 lg. can peeled tomatoes
1 lg. onion, chopped
4 cloves garlic, minced
6-10 bay leaves
½ tsp. cloves, ground
½ tsp. allspice
1 c. red wine or water
1 5 oz. bottle Spanish olives
salt and pepper to taste

Brown beef cubes in olive oil. Season to taste with salt and pepper. Pour in water, add potatoes and bring to a boil. Cover and simmer for about 1 hour. While beef is cooking, put tomatoes in blender or food processor and liquefy. Combine with onions, garlic, bay leaves, cloves and allspice in a saucepan. Bring to a boil and simmer for 30 minutes.

Combine this mixture with the beef, add the wine or water and cover and simmer for one hour longer.
Add olives and simmer uncovered for another 30 to 60 minutes or until broth has reduced and thickened to taste. Remove bay leaves before serving.

Serve over rice with pico de gallo or roll in tortillas and serve with sour cream.

BEEF STROGANOFF

1 lb. beefsteak, well trimmed
3 c. fresh mushrooms (you can used more than one type)
3 green onions, thinly sliced
6 T. olive oil
¼ tsp. thyme
¾ c. red wine or water
1 T. cornstarch
¾ c. beef broth
salt to taste
1 c. sour cream (can substitute fat free)
fresh parsley, chopped for garnish

Slice beef into thin diagonal strips. Sauté mushrooms and onions in 3 T. olive oil. Add thyme and wine or water and simmer until liquid is reduced to about ¼ cup.

Blend cornstarch into beef broth and stir into mushrooms and cook, stirring constantly until mixture boils and thickens. Keep warm.

Brown steak in remaining olive oil and sprinkle with salt. Just before serving, add browned beef and sour cream to sauce. Heat carefully, but do not boil. Sprinkle with parsley.

Serve with thin, fried noodles. Yum!!!

STUFFED FLANK STEAK

2 lb. flank steak	2 tsp. garlic, minced
2 dried chile pods	3/4 c. red wine
1 lg. sweet onion	1 tsp. thyme
1/2 c. black olives, chopped	salt and pepper to taste

Cover chiles with water in microwave safe dish, cover and cook on high for 4 minutes. Discard stems and seeds and finely chop. Sauté onion in oil until tender, about 5 minutes. Add chiles, olives, garlic, wine and thyme. Cook until wine has evaporated and stuffing is of spreading consistency.

Butterfly steak, splitting at one long edge, cutting through to center of steak. Leave opposite hinge intact. Do not completely cut through steak. Open steak and season inside with salt and pepper. Starting at one   long edge, spread stuffing evenly over half of steak. Roll up and tie roll with string every 2 inches. Season with more salt and pepper.

Brown quickly in olive oil. Transfer to roasting pan, placing seam side up. Roast for 35 to 40 minutes at 350° for rare. Let roast rest for about 10 minutes before slicing.

LAMB SHANKS ala JEANIE

4 lamb shanks
salt and pepper to taste
2 T. olive oil
2 carrots, cut into strips
1-1/2 c. celery, diced
2 tsp. parsley, chopped
1 tsp. rosemary
2 bay leaves
2 T. onion, grated
1 clove garlic, mashed
1 c. red wine or beef broth

Rub salt and pepper into shanks. Heat oil in a large skillet and add meat. Cook over medium heat until browned, turning often.

Transfer shanks to a large casserole and add vegetables. Put parsley, rosemary and bay leaves on a square of cheesecloth and tie securely. Put bag in casserole with the meat.

Combine onion, garlic and wine with drippings in the skillet. Scrape up browned bits and pour over meat in casserole. Cover and bake at 350° about 1-1/2 hours or until meat is tender. Remove herbs before serving.

BRISKET WITH ORANGE SAUCE

1 envelope onion soup mix
1-1/2 c. red wine or water
¼ c. water
2 T. flour
1 T. dried basil
½ tsp. thyme
1/3 c. orange marmalade
1-1/2 tsp. orange peel, grated
2 tsp. sugar
4 cloves garlic, minced
salt and pepper to taste
1 4# brisket of beef (trimmed of as much fat as possible)
1 lb. mushrooms, quartered

In a pan large enough to hold the brisket comfortably, combine soup mix, wine, water and flour and stir until well blended. Stir in basil, thyme, marmalade, orange peel, sugar, garlic, salt and pepper. Add brisket and spoon some of the sauce over the top.

Cover and bake at 300° for about 4 hours until tender when pierced with a fork. Reduce heat to 275° if sauce starts bubbling rapidly.

Remove brisket and pour sauce into a bowl and refrigerate until you can skim fat from sauce. Slice brisket thinly against the grain and put slices into an ovenproof dish and our sauce over meat. Top with mushrooms and baste with sauce. Cover with foil and return to oven at 325° for about 45 minutes or until heated through and mushrooms are done.

SAVORY POT ROAST

1 boneless roast beef
1 lg. onion, chopped
1 can cream of mushroom soup
1 soup can water
¼ c. brown sugar
¼ c. red wine vinegar
2 tsp. salt
1 tsp. Dijon mustard
1 T. parsley, chopped
1 tsp. Worcestershire sauce

Brown beef and onion in a large pot. Combine all other ingredients except wine and pour over beef. Cover and simmer about 1-1/2 to 3 hours. Add more water if necessary. Add wine about 15 minutes before removing from pot. Let beef cool a little before slicing. Thicken gravy if desired.

Serve with thin, fried noodles or mashed potatoes.

LANCASTER TREE

TOMATO VEGETABLE MEAT SAUCE

1 c. onion, chopped
1 c. carrots, diced
1 c. celery, diced
½ c. fennel, chopped
2 cloves garlic, minced
¾ lb. ground beef
½ lb. ground pork
salt and pepper to taste
1-1/2 c. milk
1 c. red wine or water
4 lb. tomatoes, chopped (fresh from the garden if possible)
2 T. tomato paste
3 bay leaves
3 T. Italian seasoning
olive oil

Heat oil in a large skillet and add vegetables. Sauté until soft, about 15 minutes. Stir in garlic and cook another minute. Add the meats, breaking them up. Season and cook until meat is no longer pink.

Add milk and simmer gently until the liquid is almost evaporated. This will take a while, so be patient. Stir often to prevent sticking. Add the wine and reduce, about 20 minutes.

Add tomatoes, tomato paste and seasonings, simmer over low heat for 3 to 4 hours until thick. Stir often. Remove bay leaves and cool. Chill for 24 hours to let flavors blend.

CROCKPOT CABBAGE ROLLS

12 cabbage leaves
1 lb. ground lamb (beef or turkey can be substituted)
½ c. uncooked rice
2 8 oz. cans tomato sauce
¼ c. water
½ c. red wine (or more to taste)
salt and pepper to taste
¼ tsp. thyme
¼ tsp. nutmeg
¼ tsp. cinnamon

Wash and dry cabbage leaves. Cook in microwave oven for about 20 seconds to soften so they are easy to work with.

Combine ground lamb, rice, alt, pepper, thyme, nutmeg, and cinnamon. Put 2 T. meat mixture on each leaf and roll firmly. Fasten with a toothpick or tie with baking twine.

Stack in crock-pot. Combine tomato sauce, wine and water and pour over rolls. Cover and cook on low for 8 to 10 hours.

SWEET TATERS AND SAUSAGE

2 lbs. sweet potatoes
½ c. sugar
½ c. brown sugar
¼ c. water
2 T. butter or margarine
1 lbs. sausage of choice
salt and pepper to taste

Parboil the potatoes for about 15 minutes. Peel and cut into strips. Place in a greased baking dish or Dutch over. Combine sugars, butter, salt, pepper and water. Bring to a boil and pour syrup over potatoes and bake for 45 minutes. Place sausage on top and bake for an additional 30 minutes.

This is just plain good and easy too. I don't know anyone who has tried it who doesn't like it.

COUNTRY POT ROAST WITH SOUR CREAM GRAVY

3 to 4 lb. pot roast
flour
¼ c. butter or margarine
salt and pepper to taste
1 beef bouillon cube
½ c. hot water
12 to 16 small white onions, peeled
4 lg. potatoes, peeled and quartered

Coat both sides of roast with flour. Melt butter or margarine in a large skillet and brown meat slowly. Sprinkle with salt and pepper. Dissolve bouillon cube in hot water and pour over meat. Cover and put into a preheated 350° oven. Cook 1-1/2 hours.

Add onions and potatoes and cook about 45 minutes longer or until vegetables are tender. Remove meat and vegetables and keep warm.

SOUR CREAM GRAVY:
1-1/3 c. drippings
3 T. flour
¼ c. cold water
1 c. sour cream (low fat or fat-free can be used)

Pour drippings into saucepan and blend in flour and water gradually. Cook, stirring constantly until gravy is thickened. Cook 2 minutes longer and remove from heat. Slowly stir in sour cream. Heat through but DO NOT BOIL.

APPLE PORK CHOPS

6 pork chops
3 tart cooking apples
2 c. hot water
¼ tsp. salt
¼ tsp. sage
3 T. molasses
½ tsp. salt
3 T. flour

Peel, core and slice apples. Place chops in skillet and sprinkle with salt and sage. Sauté chops until browned on both sides. Remove from skillet and reserve drippings. Place chops in a deep baking dish and cover with apples. Cover with molasses.

Make a sauce by adding flour to drippings in skillet, cool until brown. Add water slowly, balance of salt and cook until it boils. Pour over chops, cover and bake for 1 hour at 350°

What says Fall more than apples and pork chops!!

BAKED HAM & SWEET KENTUCKY BOURBON MUSTARD

½ ham, fully cooked – 6 to 9 lbs.
1 c. honey
½ c. molasses
½ c. Kentucky bourbon (or your favorite)
¼ c. orange juice
2 T. Dijon mustard

Combine honey and molasses in a pan and stir until hated. Stir in bourbon, juice and mustard.

Bake ham at 325° for about 1-1/2 hour or until meat thermometer reads 140°. Baste ham occasionally with bourbon sauce.

Transfer drippings to a pan and add remaining bourbon mixture and bring to a boil. Serve as a glaze with the sliced ham.

STUFFED PORK TENDERLOIN

6 pork tenderloin steaks, pounded to ¼ inch thick
salt and pepper to taste
¼ tsp. majoram
¼ tsp. sage
2 slices bacon, diced
1-1/4 c. toasted bread cubes
½ c. carrot, finely chopped
¼ c. onion, finely chopped
1 egg beaten
1-1/2 c. beef broth
¼ c. flour

Sprinkle flattened pork with salt, pepper, majoram and sage. Fry bacon until crisp then remove from pan. Reserve about 2 T. drippings for cooking meat. Add bread cubes, carrots, onion, egg, broth, salt and pepper to drippings in pan and mix well.

Spread stuffing on pork steaks and roll meat up and tie with strings. Roll each in flour and brown in reserved drippings. Put the rolls in a 1-1/2 qt. casserole and add broth. Cover and bake at 350° for 1-1/2 hours.

Remove strings to serve and arrange rolls on a platter and ladle some of the sauce over them. Additional sauce can be served on the side.

COUNTRY RIBS

3 lbs. country ribs
1 T. oil
1 lg. onion, sliced into ¼ to ½ inches thick

SAUCE:
1/3 c. soy sauce
1 T. mustard
2 cloves garlic, minced
2 T. cider vinegar
½ c. catsup
3 T. brown sugar
1 tsp. celery seed
salt and pepper to taste

Trim fat from ribs and brown in a large skillet. Transfer to crock-pot and put onion slices on top. Combine sauce ingredients and pour over ribs. Cover and cook on low for 8 to 10 hours

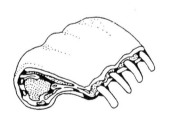

HEART

COLOMBIA

CHICKEN and VEAL RECIPES

TABLE OF CONTENTS

CHICKEN AND SWISS ROULADE

4 chicken breasts, skinned and boned
4 smoked ham slices
4 slices Swiss cheese
¼ c. chives
2 T. olive oil
1 clove garlic, crushed
¼ c. white wine or water
salt and pepper to taste
2/3 c. whipping cream

Slice three-quarters of the way, horizontally, through the breasts and open out. Cover with plastic wrap and pound with a rolling pin to flatten.

Cover each filet with a ham slice and a cheese slice. Sprinkle chives over chicken. Roll up like a jellyroll and tie to secure.

In an ovenproof pan, heat oil and cook rolls gently until browned. Pour off excess oil and add garlic, wine or water and seasonings. Cover and bake about 25 minutes until tender. Put roulades on a plate and remove string.

Put pan on high heat and boil rapidly to reduce contents, scraping up browned bits from the bottom.

Add cream and heat through. Pour sauce over breasts and serve immediately.

VEAL ELEGANTÈ

1-1/2 lb. veal, sliced about 1/3 inch thick
¼ olive oil
¼ c. onion, chopped
1 clove garlic, minced
1 T. fresh parsley, chopped
1 tsp. crumbled rosemary
salt and pepper to taste
1 small can peas (or ½ c. frozen)
½ c. white wine
1-1/2 c. fresh mushrooms, sliced
Monterey Jack cheese, grated

Brown meat on both sides, until brown. Add onions and garlic and cook slowly until onion is tender. Sprinkle with herbs and seasonings.

Lower heat and add peas, wine and mushrooms. Simmer until meat is tender. Sprinkle cheese on top and let melt. Serve immediately.

SOUR CREAM BAKED CHICKEN

6 chicken breasts, boneless and skinless
1 lb. mushrooms (any type)
flour for dredging
½ pt. sour cream
½ c. white wine or water
¼ tsp. rosemary

Shake breasts in a plastic bag with flour until coated. Brown each piece lightly in olive oil. Remove and arrange in a baking dish.

In the same skillet, brown mushrooms lightly, then add sour cream, wine or water and rosemary. Simmer the sauce, but do not boil, until smooth. Pour over chicken and bake 1 hour or until juices run clear, at 300°.

The sauce should resemble a thin white sauce.

GREEK CROSS

PORCINI CHICKEN WITH TOMATOES

1 oz. dried porcini mushrooms, soaked in warm water
for about 20 minutes
1 lg. chicken cut into 8 pieces
2 T. butter or margarine
3 T. olive oil
salt and pepper to taste
1 clove garlic, mashed
1 T. fresh rosemary (or ½ tsp. dried)
1 c. white wine or chicken broth
1 lb. ripe plum tomatoes, seeded and finely diced
2 T. fresh parsley, chopped

Drain mushrooms, reserving the liquid. Rinse mushrooms
well and mince finely. Strain the soaking water through
several layers of paper towels into a small bowl. Set both
aside.

Combine butter and oil in a large skillet that can
accommodate all the chicken pieces at once. Add chicken,
skin side down. Season with salt and pepper and cook,
turning until golden on both sides. Transfer to a platter.

Add mushrooms, garlic and rosemary to the skillet and
cook quickly for 1 minute. Add wine or water and stir to
loosen browned bits on the bottom. Cook until wine is
reduce to about half, then add the tomatoes and season
with salt. Cook for a few minutes.   (more)

(con't)

Return chicken to pot and cover with sauce. Reduce heat to low, cover and cook gently until chicken is tender, about 45 minutes. Check sauce occasionally and add mushroom liquid if sauce reduces too much. Stir in the parsley and serve.

PINOT CHICKEN

1 lg. chicken, cut into 8 pieces
1/3 c. flour
salt and pepper to taste
½ c. butter or margarine
1 c. chicken broth
¼ c. onion, minced
1/8 tsp. nutmeg, ground
½ tsp. dry mustard
1 T. celery flakes
1/2 T. hot pepper flakes
1 can cream of mushroom soup
1 can tomato sauce
1 c. water

Combine flour, salt and pepper in a plastic bag and coat each piece of chicken. Reserve flour mixture. In a heavy skillet, brown chicken in butter, then transfer to a baking dish. Pour chicken broth over chicken. Blend reserved flour mixture into butter left in skillet (add more if necessary) and add remaining ingredients. Simmer about 5 minutes and pour over chicken.

Cover dish and bake in a 350° oven for 45 minutes or until tender.

Serve over hot, buttered fettuccini.

VEAL STEW IN WINE

2 lb. veal stew meat, cut into small cubes
salt and pepper to taste
1/3 c. fresh parsley, chopped
1 clove garlic, minced finely
¾ c. white wine
1 can beef broth
1-1/4 c. water
1 4 oz. can mushrooms, undrained
1 8 oz. can small pitted olives, drained

In a large skillet, sauté veal in olive oil until browned.
Season with salt, pepper, parsley and garlic and cook for a
few minutes. Pour in wine, broth and water and cover pan.
Simmer for about 1 hour.

Add mushrooms and olives and continue simmering for
another 15 minutes. Thicken sauce with a little flour
blended with water, but keep on the thin side.

Serve over fried noodles. A fresh fruit salad goes well too.

ROSEMARY CHICKEN

1 chicken, quartered
salt and pepper to taste
1 c. white wine or water
1-1/2 T. lemon juice
1 c. vegetable oil
1 T. rosemary

Put chicken in a deep baking dish and sprinkle with salt and pepper. Combine wine or water, lemon juice, oil and rosemary. Pour over chicken and marinate overnight.

Drain chicken, saving marinade. Broil or grill chicken, turning frequently, basting often. Cook 30 minutes or until tender.

THAI CHICKEN

8 oz. chicken, cubed
2 T. olive or sesame oil
2 T. dried basil
3 T. onion, chopped finely
3 T. green pepper, chopped
1-1/2 oz. Thai chili sauce
3 oz. fish sauce

Heat oil in skillet and stir fry the chicken until no longer pink. Add basil, onion and pepper and cook until softened. Season with chili and fish sauces. Serve with white or brown rice.

STAR

PESTO CHICKEN

4 chicken breasts, boneless and skinless
½ c. pesto
½ c. cream
1 c. breadcrumbs
4 cloves garlic, unpeeled
½ c. mayonnaise
½ c. milk
salt and pepper to taste
2 T. lime juice

Pound breasts to flatten and spread 2 T. pesto on each.
Roll and seal with a toothpick. Dip roll in milk and coat
with breadcrumbs. Place chicken and garlic in a 350° oven
in an oiled pan and bake for 30 minutes. Remove garlic for
use in the sauce and continue cooking chicken for another
15 minutes.

SAUCE: Squeeze garlic into pan and add mayonnaise,
milk, lemon juice and salt and pepper and cook over low
heat. Stir constantly until warmed. Put cooked chicken on
a plate and pour sauce over them.

Serve with seasoned rice and a white merlot.

CREAMY BASIL CHICKEN

1 lb. fettuccine, cooked
1 lb. chicken, boneless and skinless, cubed
1 c. onions, minced
¾ lb, mushrooms, sliced
1 T. olive oil
3 T. butter or margarine
3 T. flour
2 c. chicken broth
1 c. whipping cream
2 tsp. dried basil, crumbled
salt and pepper to taste

Sauté chicken, onions and mushrooms in oil until browned. In a saucepan, melt butter or margarine and stir in flour until smooth, add broth and cream and stir in basil, salt and pepper. Bring to a boil and stir constantly. Add chicken mixture and warm through. Serve over fettuccine.

DEE'S CHICKEN TETRAZINI

1 small pkg. spaghetti, cooked
4 c. cooked chicken, diced
¼ c. pimento
¼ c. parsley
¼ c. red or green bell pepper, finely chopped
¼ c. onion, chopped
2 cans cream of mushroom soup
¼ c. cheddar cheese, grated
1 c. chicken broth
sautéed fresh mushrooms, (optional)

Combine all ingredients and bake for 1 hour or microwave for 20 minutes.

This is a fast, simple dinner that can be made ahead of time.

COQ AU VIN
(for crock-pot)

2-1/2 lb. frying chicken, cut into 8 pieces
6 bacon slices, diced
2/3 c. green onions, sliced
8 small white onions, peeled
½ lb. whole mushrooms
1 clove garlic, crushed
salt and pepper to taste
½ tsp. dry thyme
8 small new potatoes, scrubbed
1 c. chicken broth
1 c. red wine or water
chopped parsley (for garnish)

In a large skillet, cook bacon and green onions until bacon is crisp. Remove and drain on paper towels. Add chicken pieces to skillet and brown well on all sides.

Remove chicken when browned and set aside. Put peeled onions, mushrooms and garlic in crock-pot. Add browned chicken pieces, bacon and green onions, salt, pepper, thyme, potatoes and chicken broth. Cover and cook on low 8 to 10 hours. During the last 30 minutes, add wine and cook on high.

When serving, sprinkle with chopped parsley.

SEAFOOD RECIPES

GEOMETRIC

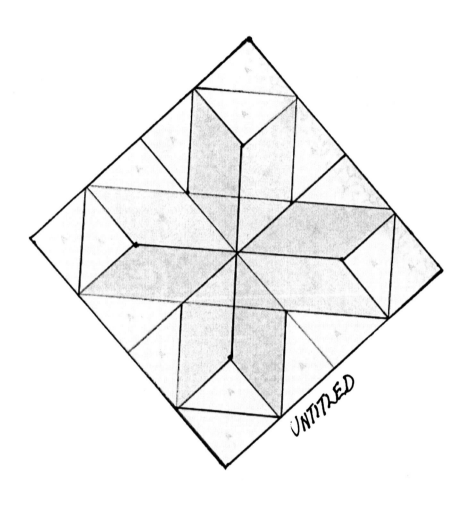

UNTITLED

154

TABLE OF CONTENTS

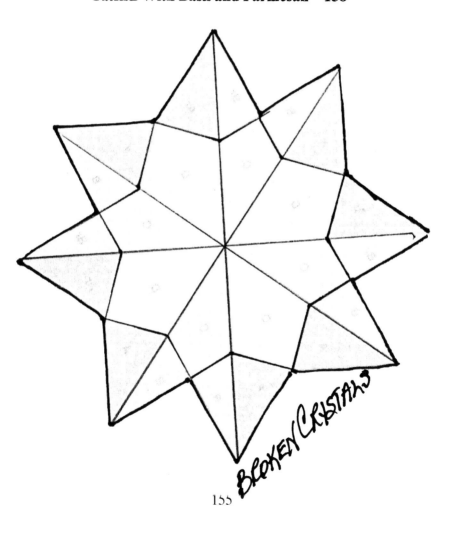

GRILLED RED SNAPPER WITH HERBS AND WINE

6 6 oz. red snapper filets
¾ c. extra virgin olive oil
1 c. white wine or apple juice
2 med. shallots, minced
3 T. chives, minced
2 T. fresh parsley, chopped
1 T. thyme, minced
1 T. lemon zest
salt and pepper to taste

Combine all ingredients, except fish. Place fish in a glass baking dish and cover with 2/3 of the marinade. Cover and refrigerate for about 30 to 45 minutes.

Remove fish from refrigerator and let stand at room temperature. Light the grill and oil the grate. Remove fish from marinade and put on grill. Cook 4 minutes per side or until fish flakes. Transfer to a serving plate and serve with the remaining marinade, which has been warmed.

EAST COAST FISH STEW

1 T. olive oil
1 clove garlic, minced
½ c. onion, chopped
1/3 c. green bell pepper, chopped
¼ lb. mushrooms, sliced
2 c. tomatoes, chopped
¾ c. tomato paste
½ c. water
1 c. chicken broth
1 T. lemon juice
1 bay leaf
1 tsp. oregano
1 tsp. sugar
salt and pepper to taste
1-1/2 lb. white fish of choice

Sauté garlic, onion, pepper and mushrooms until browned. Add tomatoes, tomato paste, broth, water, juice and seasonings.

Cook until heated through. Add fish, which has been cut into large pieces and cook until it flakes easily, about 10 to 15 minutes.

Serve over rice or spaghetti.

CATFISH WITH BASIL AND PARMESAN

1/3 c. dry bread crumbs
4 T. Parmesan cheese
1-1/2 tsp. dry basil
½ tsp. paprika
fresh parsley, chopped for garnish
4 catfish filets, or other fish filets of choice
¼ c. milk
salt and pepper to taste

Combine all ingredients except fish, milk and parsley. Dip filets in milk and coat with crumb mixture. Spray a baking dish with cooking spray and place fish in pan.

Bake in a 375° oven until fish flakes easily. Sprinkle with parsley.

DESSERTS

CUBE LATTICE

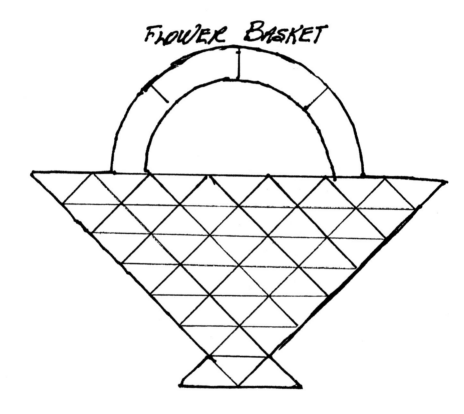

FLOWER BASKET

TABLE OF CONTENTS

RAISIN CAKE

½ c. red wine
½ c. brandy
2 c. golden raisins
½ c. butter or margarine, softened
1-1/2 c. sugar
2 eggs
1-1/2 c. applesauce
3 c. flour, sifted
¼ c. cocoa
1-1/2 tsp. baking soda
1 tsp. each, salt, cinnamon
¼ tsp. ground cloves

Combine wine, brandy and raisins in a saucepan, cover
and simmer over low heat about 5 minutes. Remove
and let cool. Cream butter and sugar until creamy, beat
in eggs and applesauce. Sift in flour and all dry
ingredients.

Add dry ingredients to batter and beat until smooth.
Stir in raisins and liquid. Spoon into a well-greased
tube pan, bottom-lined with parchment paper and bake
at 350° for 65 minutes or until done.

Remove from oven and cool before taking from pan.
Cool on a rack and dust top with powdered sugar or a
sugar glaze.

A good holiday cake!

HONEY PIE

1 T. unflavored gelatin
½ c. hot water
1-1/4 oz. vanilla pudding (not instant)
1-1/2 c. milk
½ tsp. cinnamon
¼ c. honey
1 c. heavy cream
1 9-inch pie shell, baked
1 c. peanut brittle, crushed

Dissolve gelatin in hot water. Prepare pudding mix as directed on package, using 1-1/2 c. milk. Remove filling from heat and add softened gelatin, stir until dissolved. Stir in cinnamon and honey.

Cool completely, about 1 hour. Fold in cream that has been whipped until stiff. Spoon in pie shell and cover top with crushed peanut brittle.

Chill several hours or overnight.

RICE PUDDING

¾ c. quick cooking rice
¾ c. hot water
½ tsp. orange peel, grated
1 3-1/4 oz. pkg. regular vanilla pudding
¼ tsp. salt
1 c. milk
1 T. cinnamon
1 c. whipping cream

Combine rice, water and orange peel and bring to a boil. Remove from heat and cover. Let stand 10 minutes.

Add pudding mix, salt, cinnamon and mil. Cook, stirring until mixture comes to a boil and thickens. Remove from heat and cool. Cover and refrigerate until ready to serve and is well chilled.

When ready to serve, fold in whipping cream and spoon into dishes.

PATCHWORK COBBLER

1 c. shortening
1-1/2 c. sugar
3 eggs
3 T. milk
4 c. flour
½ tsp. baking soda
a few slices fresh bread, torn into small pieces
2 cans (15 oz. ea.) pie filling, any flavor

Combine shortening, sugar, eggs, milk, flour and
baking soda and mix well. Lightly oil a 13x19 inch pan
and sprinkle bottom with the bread pieces. Put half of
dough on top of pieces and pat gently to cover.

Put filling over the dough and put patches of remaining
dough over top. Sprinkle with sugar. Bake at 350° for
45 minutes to 1 hour or until lightly browned.

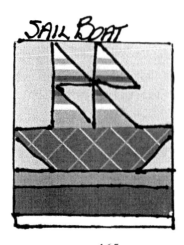

165

CHERRY CRISP

the Very Best can use other fillings.

2 cans cherry pie filling
2 sticks butter or margarine
1 pkg. white cake mix
1-1/4 c. pecans, chopped

Put pie filling in bottom of cake pan. Sprinkle cake mix over top. DO NOT STIR! Top with nuts and pour melted butter over the top. Bake for 30 minutes at 350°.

Made in "2" 9-in Pans.
Bake ea. syperatly at 360⁰ for 40.min
Center Rack
or untill
Crisp Brown on top.

APPLE DUMPLINGS

4 to 6 apples, peeled and thinly sliced
1 c. Bisquick
1/3 c. milk
1 c. water
1 c. sugar
1 T. cinnamon

Combine apples, Bisquick and milk. Put into a greased baking dish. In the meantime, bring water, sugar and cinnamon to a boil and pour over dry mixture.

Bake for 25 minutes at 425°. Slice when cool.

These are good for breakfast on a cold, snowy morning.

SWEET TATER PIE

2 lbs. sweet potatoes, peeled and sliced
½ c. butter or margarine
3 lg. eggs
1 c. sugar
½ c. sweetened condensed milk
1 tsp. nutmeg
1 tsp. vanilla
1 tsp. lemon extract
1 pkg. frozen deep-dish piecrusts, thawed

Cook sweet potatoes in boiling water about 30 minutes or until fork tender, drain.

Beat potatoes and butter until smooth. Add eggs and next 5 ingredients and mix well. Pour mixture into 2 piecrusts.

Bake at 350° for about 45 minutes or until a knife inserted in center comes out clean. Cool before serving.

This is an old southern favorite made simpler with frozen piecrusts. You can use your own recipe for crusts, of course.

MISCELLANEOUS

STYLIZED ROSE

TABLE OF CONTENTS

HOT WINE CRANBERRY PUNCH

2 1 pt. bottles cranberry juice cocktail
2 c. water
1-1/2 c. sugar
4 sticks of cinnamon
12 whole cloves
peel of ½ lemon
2 bottles red wine
¼ c. lemon juice

Combine all ingredients in a saucepan except wine and lemon juice. Bring to a boil and stir until sugar is dissolved. Simmer gently about 20 minutes, then strain.

Combine syrup with wine and lemon juice and heat but do not boil. Serve in mugs with a sprinkling of nutmeg.

This is a good holiday drink or one for a cold winter night.

STRAWBERRY PUNCH

2 pts. fresh strawberries
1-1/2 c. sugar
3 c. water
1-1/2 c. lemon juice
2 c. sparkling wine
mint for garnish

Puree strawberries in a food processor or blender and sieve to remove seeds.

Combine sugar and water in a saucepan and heat slowly until sugar dissolves.

Combine with strawberry puree and lemon juice and then add wine. Chill thoroughly. Garnish with fresh mint.

This is a great punch to serve at bridal showers.

BLACK CHERRY BBQ SAUCE

¾ c. black cherry soda
1 17 oz. can Bing cherries, drained
3 T. cherry preserves
2 T fresh lemon juice, or to taste
2 T. butter or margarine
1 T. sugar, or to taste
½ tsp. cinnamon
¼ c. apple juice
1 T. cornstarch
Kosher or coarse salt and ground black pepper to taste

Combine cherry soda, preserves, lemon juice, butter, sugar, cinnamon and 3 T. apple juice in a saucepan and bring to a boil over high heat. Reduce heat to medium and let the sauce simmer gently for 5 minutes.

Combine the remaining juice and the cornstarch in a small bowl and stir to form thick paste. Whisk into the cherry sauce. Bring sauce to boil over high heat to thicken, about 1 minute.

Taste for seasoning, adding more sugar or lemon juice to adjust sweetness and add salt and pepper to taste. This should be highly seasoned. Can be served warm or at room temperature. Sauce can be refrigerated, covered for about 1 week.

Try over chicken, lamb or pork.

CHEESEY BASIL CAKE

1 T. butter or margarine
½ c. bread crumbs
1/3 c. Parmesan cheese
¼ c. dried basil
¼ c. olive oil
½ c. parsley
Salt to taste

1 clove garlic
1 lb. ricotta cheese, room
   temperature
2 lbs. cream cheese, room
   temperature
½ lb. Parmesan cheese
   grated
5 eggs
½ c. pecans, lightly roasted

Spray bottom and sides of a 10" spring form pan. Mix breadcrumbs and ¼ c. Parmesan cheese and sprinkle into pan. Turn pan to coat.

Combine basil, parsley, oil, salt and garlic in a blender or food processor until a paste forms. Put ricotta, cream cheese and Parmesan in a mixer bowl and mix until smooth. Add eggs.

Remove 1/3 of this mixture into a small bowl. Into the remainder, fold in the basil mixture and mix until well blended. Pour into the prepared pan and spread an even layer of the cheese mixture on top. Sprinkle with chopped pecans. Put pan on a baking sheet and bake 1-1/2 hours at 325°. Turn off oven and cool cake about 1 hour in oven with the slightly ajar. Remove and cool completely. Serve at room temperature.

RIPE OLIVE AND CHARRED ONION SALSA

3 med. sweet onions, skin on, halved
1/4 c. olive oil
1/4 c. balsamic vinegar
1 T. white wine vinegar
1 tsp. red pepper flakes
1 c. whole, pitted ripe olives
2 tsp. oregano

Place onion halves, cut side down in a shallow pan. Bake in a 425°degree oven for 30 minutes or until onions are slightly soft and cut sides are blackened.

 When cool enough to handle, discard skins and trim stems. Put onions in food processor or blender with oil, vinegars and red pepper flakes. Process in 2 or 3 second bursts or just until coarsely chopped. Add olives and oregano and process 2 to 4 seconds until just chopped.

QUILTERS ORANGE SPICE BREAKFAST OR BRUNCH BREW

9 cups water
9 individual size orange and spice herbal tea bags
8 whole cloves
12 whole allspice
peel from ½ orange, cut into small strips
2 cups water
1 (12 oz.) can frozen orange juice concentrate, thawed and undiluted
½ c. lemon juice
¼ c. honey
1/3 c. sugar
2 oranges, sliced thin

Remove tags from tea bags. Fill 12 cup electric coffee maker with 9 cups of water. Combine next 4 ingredients in coffee basket. Perk through a complete cycle.

When cycle is complete, add the remaining ingredients, except orange slices, to tea mixture. Stir. Pour into cups and float an orange slice in each cup.

This recipe is from my friend Matilda de Nada. Thanks so much!!

Glossary

Appliqué – Technique used to stitch small pieces of cut out fabric to a larger piece of fabric usually in a planned pattern or design.

Backing – Bottom layer or back of a quilted item.

Batting – Also called filler. A non-woven material used for the middle layer of a quilted item. Comes in standard and smaller craft sizes.

Binding – Fabric sewn around the outer edges of a quilt.

Block – A pieced, appliquéd or quilted section containing a complete design. It doesn't have to be a specific shape and may be a tiny section or large enough to cover an entire bed.

Blocking/Pressing - This is recommended before and after blocks or sections are sewn together.

Border – The outer section of a quilt surrounding the central area. Often used to enlarge a quilt. The border may be appliquéd, pieced or quilted or may also be omitted.

Comforter – A type of quilt usually overstuffed. Tufting instead of quilting often holds layers together. This is known as a tied quilt.

Crazy Quilt - An American design using odd shapes and a variety of fabrics sewn together like a jigsaw puzzle

Dividers - Strips of fabric set between blocks, if desired. It is a combination of blocks and dividers sewn together with or without a border for the top a quilt.

Marking – The method used to draw outlines of pieces to be appliquéd on a block or quilt in order to insure the proper placement. Method also used to draw a quilting stitch pattern on a quilt top.

Miter – A diagonal seam sewn at a 45° angle from the inside of a corner to the outside of a corner or binding at each of the four corners of a quilt. A well-mitered corner will form a 90° angle.

Patch/Piece – A small section of cloth. Also pieced as sewing small sections of cloth together.

Quilting – A method of sewing that enjoys a running stitch in a decorative design. Three layers of cloth are connected. This is to prevent batting from shifting.

Rolling - The process of winding the finished section of a quilt onto a quilting frame.

Setting – The process of joining completed blocks together to form a quilt top.

Template – A cutting pattern made from paper or other material to outline designs on fabric.

Equipment

Assembling all the equipment you will need is an important first step. The following are small items but very necessary, the larger items are optional and may not be necessary depending on the items you plan to make.

Art Eraser – Your quilting stitches don't always cover the quilting lines that have been drawn on the quilt top. This eraser will take them off.

Batting (filler) – This is a non-woven material used between the top and bottom fabric.

Bias binding – A bias cut fabric strip usually sewn around the edges of a finished quilt or other items. It can be purchased readymade or cut from the fabric on hand.

Compass – Used for designing your own templates.

Graph Paper – This is used for enlarging or reducing patterns.

Fabric – Fabric should be washed gently by hand before using. Press on wrong side with grain. Press blocks before they are sewn together. Completed top should be blocked before it is attached to batting and back. *Remember, creases cannot be removed from fabric after it has been quilted. A finished quilt should never be ironed.*

Marking materials – Always use a dressmaker's pencil, carbon paper, or tailors chalk to trace a design. Using other pencils will not wash out.

Needles – You will need a variety of needles to complete your project. Needles that are the correct size and length are called "between" needles. Experienced quilters often use a No. 9 one-inch needle.

Pin Cushion – Use rust proof pins and keep them in a handy pincushion.

Template Materials – Stiff paper, plastic, sandpaper are often used to make an accurate pattern. Fine sandpaper is an excellent material because it will not slip then tracing a pattern. Plastic is used for templates that can be used over and over again.

Sewing Machine – A sewing machine can be used to make all or part of a quilted item.

Scissors – Various kinds of scissors should be used for different jobs. Never use fabric-cutting scissors on paper; it dulls them.

Thread – If quilt is done in cotton, quilting thread should be cotton. Thread color should be related to the theme of the quilted item.

Wax – Wax is a strengthener and if the thread is pulled over the wax it will keep it from snarling and twisting and make it stronger.

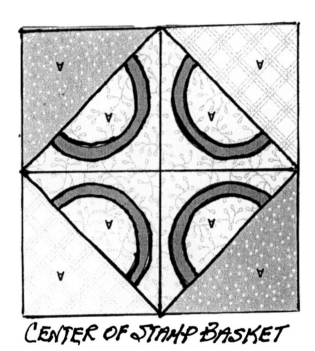

CENTER OF STAMP BASKET

To Order Copies

Please send me _____ copies of *The Quilters' Cookbook* at $11.95 each plus $3.75 S/H. (Make checks payable to Hearts 'N Tummies Ckbk. Co.)

Name _____

Street _____

City _____ State _____ Zip _____

HEARTS 'N TUMMIES COOKBOOK CO.
3544 Blakslee Street
Wever IA   52658
1-800-571-2665

To Order Copies

Please send me _____ copies of *The Quilters' Cookbook* at $11.95 each plus $3.75 S/H. (Make checks payable to Hearts 'N Tummies Ckbk. Co.)

Name _____

Street _____

City _____ State _____ Zip _____

HEARTS 'N TUMMIES COOKBOOK CO.
3544 Blakslee Street
Wever IA   52658
1-800-571-2665